GOOD TALK

ALSO BY
MIRA JACOB

THE SLEEPWALKER'S GUIDE
TO DANCING

GOOD TALK

A MEMOIR IN CONVERSATIONS

MIRA JACOB

RANDOM HOUSE · NEW YORK

PUBLISHED IN THE UNITED STATES BY RANDOM HOUSE, AN IMPRINT AND DIVISION OF PENGUIN RANDOM HOUSE LLC, NEW YORK.

RANDOM HOUSE AND THE HOUSE COLOPHON ARE REGISTERED TRADEMARKS OF PENGUIN RANDOM HOUSE LLC.

PHOTO CREDITS ARE LOCATED ON PAGES 353–55.

LIBRARY OF CONGRESS CATALOGING-IN-PUBLICATION DATA
NAMES: JACOB, MIRA.
TITLE: GOOD TALK: A MEMOIR IN CONVERSATIONS / MIRA JACOB.
DESCRIPTION: FIRST EDITION. | NEW YORK: RANDOM HOUSE, 2018.
IDENTIFIERS: LCCN 2017021147 | ISBN 9780399589041 (ACID-FREE PAPER) | ISBN 9780399589058 (EBOOK)
SUBJECTS: LCSH: JACOB, MIRA. | WOMEN AUTHORS, AMERICAN—BIOGRAPHY. | ASIAN AMERICAN AUTHORS—BIOGRAPHY.
CLASSIFICATION: LCC PS3610.A356415 Z46 2018 | DDC 813/.6 [B]—DC23
LC RECORD AVAILABLE AT HTTPS://LCCN.LOC.GOV/2017021147

PRINTED IN CHINA ON ACID-FREE PAPER

RANDOMHOUSEBOOKS.COM

246897531

FIRST EDITION

BOOK DESIGN BY PETE FRIEDRICH, PAGETURNER GRAPHIC NOVELS

FOR J AND Z:
YOU ARE MY COUNTRY.

GOOD TALK

CHAPTER 1: 2014

6-YEAR-OLD + MICHAEL JACKSON OBSESSION = A LOT OF QUESTIONS.
WHO TAUGHT HIM TO DANCE?
IS THAT HOW PEOPLE REALLY WALK ON THE MOON?
WHAT IS THE JACKSON 5?
IS HIS SKIN LIKE MY SKIN?
WHAT IS A LA TOYA?
DID HE LOSE HIS OTHER GLOVE?
IS HIS HAIR LIKE MY HAIR?
0 7464-35745-1
Epic

AT FIRST THEY WERE PRETTY BASIC...
Thriller
WHO IS BETTER, MICHAEL JACKSON OR MICHAEL JORDAN?
THAT'S APPLES AND ORANGES.
NO, MICHAEL JACKSON IS A HUMAN SINGER AND MICHAEL JORDAN IS A HUMAN—
OMYGODSTOP! MICHAEL JACKSON!
...AND THEN THEY WEREN'T.

WAS MICHAEL JACKSON BROWN OR WAS HE WHITE?
WELL, HE WAS BLACK, BUT HIS SKIN WAS BROWN AND THEN IT...TURNED WHITE.
HE TURNED WHITE?
YES.
ARE YOU GOING TO TURN WHITE?
NO.
AM I GOING TO—
NO.
DADDY?
DADDY'S ALREADY WHITE.
BUT WAS HE ALWAYS?

I'M EAST INDIAN AND MY HUSBAND IS JEWISH. WE'VE LIVED ON THE SAME BLOCK IN BROOKLYN FOR ALMOST TWO DECADES. A LOT OF MIXED-RACE KIDS LIVE ON OUR BLOCK. A LOT OF EVERYBODY LIVES ON OUR BLOCK.
DO I LOOK LIKE NICK?
A LITTLE? HE'S BLACK AND RUSSIAN.
WHAT ABOUT CLAUDINE?
SHE'S KOREAN AND CHINESE.
WHAT ABOUT THE GUY ON THE CORNER WHO IS ALWAYS FALLING ASLEEP WHILE HE'S STANDING?
THE WHO?!
OH. YEAH. NOPE, YOU DON'T LOOK LIKE HIM EITHER.

FOREVER, MICHAEL
INDIANS ARE NOT VERY COOL.
THAT'S NOT TRUE. LOOK AT BOLLYWOOD.
WHAT?
AND MINDY KALING!
WHO?
GANDHI. GANDHI IS SUPER COOL.
WHAT DID HE SING?

WE'RE ALMOST THERE
WE'VE GOT FOREVER
JUST A LITTLE BIT OF YOU
YOU ARE THERE
DAPPER-DAN
DEAR MICHAEL
I'LL COME HOME TO YOU
CAN I MAKE MY HAIR LIKE MICHAEL'S?
NO.
WHY NOT?
BECAUSE THAT'S CULTURAL APPROPRIATION.
WHAT?
THAT'S USING SOMEONE ELSE'S ETHNICITY TO MAKE A FASHION STATEMENT.
WHAT?
YOU'LL LOOK SILLY.
OH, OKAY.

MOMMY, I HAVE CHANGED MY NAME TO "THE SIXTH JACKSON."
WAIT, REALLY? I'M SUPPOSED TO SAY, "THIS IS MY SON, THE SIXTH JACKSON"?
NO. JUST SAY, "THIS IS THE SIXTH JACKSON," AND THEN I WILL SHOW THEM MY MOVES AND THEN THEY WILL UNDERSTAND.
DAMN.

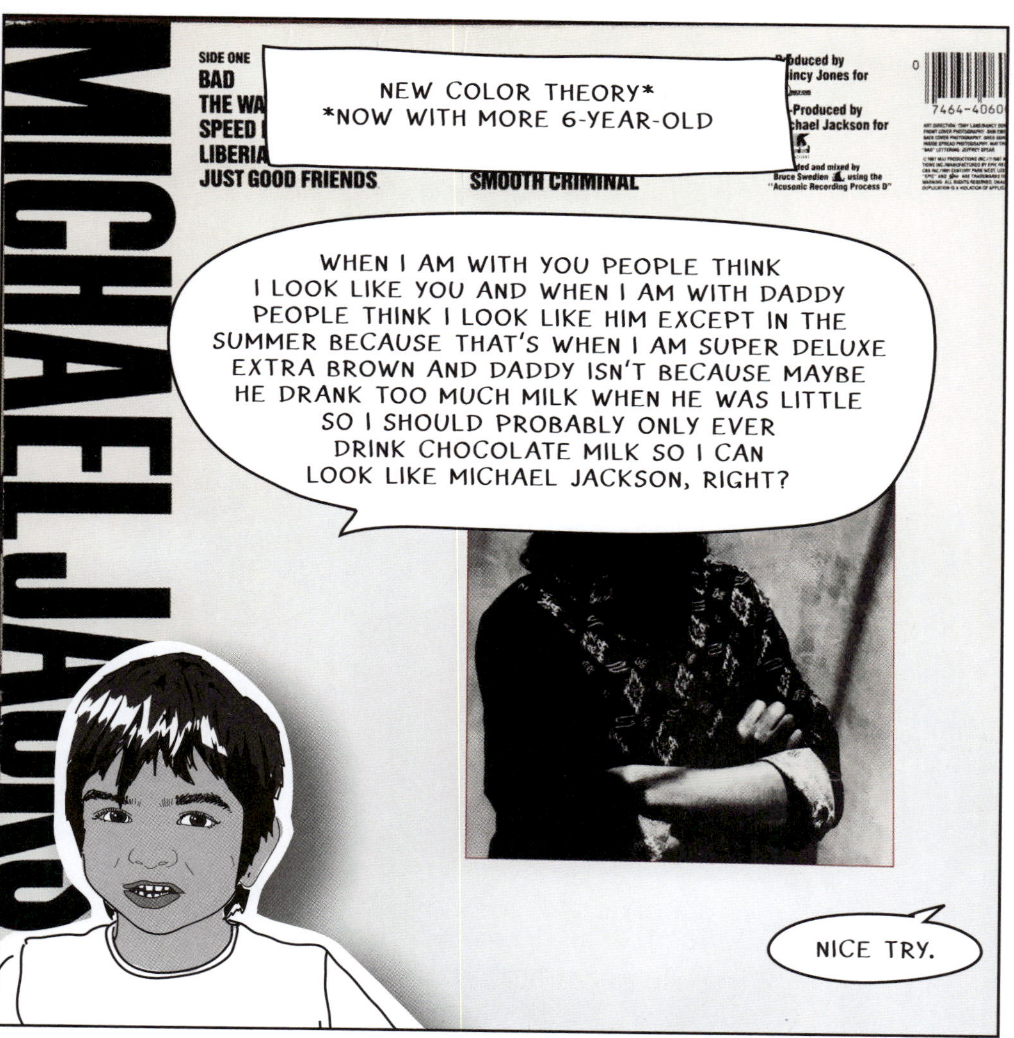

NEW COLOR THEORY*
*NOW WITH MORE 6-YEAR-OLD
SIDE ONE
BAD
JUST GOOD FRIENDS
SMOOTH CRIMINAL
WHEN I AM WITH YOU PEOPLE THINK I LOOK LIKE YOU AND WHEN I AM WITH DADDY PEOPLE THINK I LOOK LIKE HIM EXCEPT IN THE SUMMER BECAUSE THAT'S WHEN I AM SUPER DELUXE EXTRA BROWN AND DADDY ISN'T BECAUSE MAYBE HE DRANK TOO MUCH MILK WHEN HE WAS LITTLE SO I SHOULD PROBABLY ONLY EVER DRINK CHOCOLATE MILK SO I CAN LOOK LIKE MICHAEL JACKSON, RIGHT?
NICE TRY.

WHAT DID MICHAEL JACKSON LIKE BEING BETTER, BROWN OR WHITE?
UM. HE LIKED BOTH.
BAD
BUT WHAT DID HE LIKE BETTER?
NEITHER.
BUT WHAT—
CAN WE PLEASE STOP TALKING ABOUT THIS?
WHAT COLOR WAS HE WHEN HE SANG "MAN IN THE MIRROR"?

Xscape
I'M GOING TO TURN MYSELF WHITE!
NO, YOU CANNOT DECIDE TO BE WHITE. IT DOESN'T WORK LIKE THAT.
AND I WILL HAVE RED LIPS AND MY NOSE WILL LOOK LIKE IT'S FALLING OFF AND I WILL SCARE KIDS EVEN THOUGH I LOVE THEM!
NOPE.

EVERY TIME Z ASKED ME A QUESTION, I WOULD REMEMBER ALL THE TIMES I HAD ASKED SIMILAR QUESTIONS GROWING UP. ALL THE THINGS I'D BEEN TOLD. ALL THE THINGS THAT STILL DIDN'T MAKE SENSE.
WHY?
WHY?
BUT WHY?
WHY?
WHY?
WHY?

IN AUGUST, AN UNARMED TEENAGER NAMED MICHAEL BROWN WAS SHOT AND KILLED BY A MISSOURI COP. BY FALL, PROTESTS AGAINST POLICE BRUTALITY WERE SHUTTING DOWN THE STREETS OF NEW YORK.
IS IT BAD TO BE BROWN?
WHAT? NO! IT'S GREAT BEING BROWN! WE LOOK GOOD IN COLORS! WE HAVE HISTORY! WE DON'T GET SKIN CANCER AS EASILY!
WHY ARE YOU YELLING AT ME?
I DON'T KNOW!

THE TV SAID THE POLICE KILLED A KID NAMED FERGUSON BECAUSE HE WAS BROWN.
HIS NAME WAS *MICHAEL BROWN.* HE WAS BLACK. HE WAS KILLED IN A TOWN CALLED FERGUSON.
EASONS GR
BY A WHITE POLICE?
POLICEMAN. YES.
FERGUSON IS FAR AWAY, RIGHT?

ARE WHITE PEOPLE AFRAID OF BROWN PEOPLE?
SOMETIMES.
HOW DO YOU KNOW?
WHAT?
HOW DO YOU KNOW WHICH ONES ARE AFRAID OF YOU?
INVINCIB
MOMMY HOW DO YOU—
YOU DON'T ALWAYS.

IS DADDY AFRAID OF US?
NO.
NO.
MOVLP013

WAIT, HE ASKED YOU THAT? IF I WAS AFRAID OF HIM?
SO I TOLD HIM NO, AND THAT SOMETIMES THE NEWS IS HARD TO UNDERSTAND AND—
OUR SON?
WHAT?
OUR SON ASKED IF I WAS AFRAID OF HIM?
YES.
WHAT DO WE DO?
I DON'T KNOW.

SOMETIMES, YOU DON'T KNOW HOW CONFUSED YOU ARE ABOUT SOMETHING IMPORTANT UNTIL YOU TRY EXPLAINING IT TO SOMEONE ELSE.

FOR YEARS I HAD BEEN TELLING MYSELF THAT AMERICA WAS CHANGING FOR THE BETTER, AND THAT THE PAIN AND CONFUSION I'D FELT GROWING UP HERE WOULD SOON BE A THING OF THE PAST. HADN'T WE JUST ELECTED OUR FIRST BLACK PRESIDENT? DIDN'T THAT MEAN THOSE OF US WHO'D ALWAYS BEEN TREATED LIKE WE WERE SUSPICIOUS, OR INVISIBLE, OR JUST LUCKY TO BE ALLOWED IN, WERE FINALLY GOING TO FEEL LIKE WE WERE SAFE AND WELCOME AND LOVED?

NOW EVERY QUESTION Z ASKED MADE ME REALIZE THE GROWING GAP BETWEEN THE AMERICA I'D BEEN RAISED TO BELIEVE IN AND THE ONE RISING FAST ALL AROUND US. I KEPT THINKING IF I COULD GO BACK IN TIME AND MAKE SENSE OF THE THINGS I'D BEEN TOLD GROWING UP, I WOULD BE ABLE TO GIVE Z BETTER ANSWERS, MAYBE EVEN FIND A WAY TOWARD THAT BETTER COUNTRY. SOON THOUGH, WITH NEWS OF THE BLACK LIVES MATTER MOVEMENT FLOODING OUR TELEVISIONS, AND THE RISE OF DONALD TRUMP, I WOULD HAVE JUST AS MANY QUESTIONS AS HE DID.

CHAPTER 2: INDIANS IN AMERICA

NO MATTER HOW MANY TIMES I HEARD ABOUT HOW MY PARENTS MET AND MARRIED, IT DIDN'T MAKE SENSE.
I MET YOUR FATHER IN JANUARY 1968. WE MARRIED IN BOMBAY THE NEXT MONTH. WE ARRIVED IN AMERICA THE END OF MARCH.
JUST LIKE THAT?
WHAT JUST LIKE THAT? THAT'S HOW EVERYONE DID IT.
MY FATHER WAS ALWAYS A LITTLE BETTER WITH THE DETAILS.
I WANTED TO COME TO AMERICA TO STUDY OPEN-HEART SURGERY BUT MY MOTHER SAID SHE WOULDN'T LET ME GO UNLESS I MARRIED SOMEONE FROM HOME, SO I LOOKED THROUGH A STACK OF PICTURES AND SAID, "HER AND NO ONE ELSE."
WHY HER?
HAVE YOU SEEN THAT PICTURE?

THAT PICTURE
I CAME HOME FROM COLLEGE ONE DAY AND MY PARENTS SAID, "DADDY'S JOB HAS BEEN TRANSFERRED TO ITALY. WE ARE MOVING. YOU ARE NOT COMING WITH US. YOU WILL GET MARRIED."
WE WENT AND HAD THIS PICTURE TAKEN AND SENT IT OUT.
WE DIDN'T WANT HER IN THE DANGEROUS HANDS OF ITALIAN MEN.
MY GRANDMOTHER'S VERSION OF THE STORY

WIKIPEDIA WILL TELL YOU CHRISTIANITY CAME TO INDIA IN THE SECOND OR THIRD CENTURY. MOST WESTERNERS ASSUME IT CAME WITH BRITISH COLONIZATION.
IT MOST CERTAINLY DID NOT!
MY PARENTS ARE SYRIAN CHRISTIAN. SYRIAN CHRISTIANS WILL TELL YOU CHRISTIANITY CAME TO INDIA AROUND 52 A.D. WITH THE ARRIVAL OF SAINT THOMAS.

TO FIND A MATCH FOR MY MOTHER, HER PARENTS PUT THE WORD OUT AMONG THEIR COMMUNITY, AND SEVERAL YOUNG MEN, INCLUDING MY FATHER, CAME TO MEET HER.

HERE IS THE THING: USUALLY, ALL THE PARENTS WILL LEAVE SO THE TWO WILL HAVE A LITTLE TIME TO TALK ALONE, BUT WHEN WE MET, OUR PARENTS WOULDN'T LEAVE THE ROOM. AFTERWARD, OUTSIDE, I YELLED! I SAID, "WHO IS GETTING MARRIED, YOU OR ME?" MY MOTHER SAID, "IF YOU MARRY HER, YOU WILL HAVE PLENTY OF TIME TO TALK ALONE."

ALL OF YOUR PARENTING SKILLS SUDDENLY MAKE SENSE.

SO WHEN DID YOU AND MOM TALK FOR THE FIRST TIME?

AFTER WE MARRIED.

YOU'VE GOT TO BE KIDDING.

WE WROTE LETTERS!

SHE TOLD ME SHE WAS 5'7".

I DON'T REMEMBER THAT.

5'4"

MY MOM WAS RAISED IN THE CITY OF MUMBAI. MY FATHER WAS RAISED IN A SMALL TOWN NEAR CHENNAI. NEITHER OF MY PARENTS HAD EVER LEFT INDIA. THEY FLEW FROM MUMBAI TO ROME TO LONDON TO NEW YORK.
AT THE HOTEL IN ROME, YOUR MOTHER PUSHED A BUTTON AND A LITTLE ROOM OPENED. I WENT IN BUT BEFORE SHE COULD, THE DOOR CLOSED AND WOULDN'T OPEN. I PUSHED EVERY BUTTON I COULD FIND! THE LITTLE ROOM SHOOK AND SHOOK AND WHEN IT FINALLY OPENED, I WAS SOMEWHERE I HAD NEVER BEEN AND YOUR MOTHER HAD COMPLETELY DISAPPEARED!!!

ARCTIC CIRCLE
TROPIC OF CANCER
ELEVATOR.

MY PARENTS ARRIVED IN BOSTON ON MARCH 28, 1968. ONE WEEK LATER, THEY WERE AT A DINNER PARTY WHEN THEY HEARD THE NEWS.

IN APRIL THEY FLEW INTO ALBUQUERQUE. THEY WERE THE THIRD INDIAN FAMILY TO MOVE INTO THE STATE.*
I HAD READ EVERY LOUIS L'AMOUR BOOK AND KNEW ABOUT COWBOYS AND INDIANS AND HOLD-'EM-UPS, SO I WAS EXCITED.
I LOOKED DOWN AND SAW NOTHING BUT BROWN, BROWN, BROWN. THERE WERE ONLY A FEW PAVED ROADS. IT WAS LIKE LANDING ON MARS.
*SOURCE: THE FIRST TWO FAMILIES

MY BROTHER WAS BORN NINE MONTHS AFTER THEY GOT TO ALBUQUERQUE. I WAS BORN FOUR YEARS LATER, AND ONE MONTH PREMATURE.

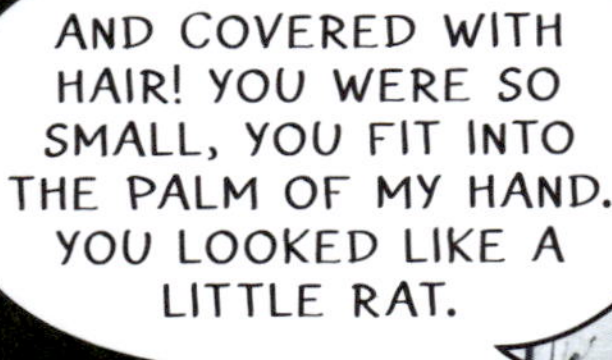

AND COVERED WITH HAIR! YOU WERE SO SMALL, YOU FIT INTO THE PALM OF MY HAND. YOU LOOKED LIKE A LITTLE RAT.

DAD!
WHAT? WE KEPT YOU, UGLY THING.

MY MOTHER'S STORIES FROM THIS TIME ARE ALWAYS A LITTLE WILD AND UNSETTLING.

ONCE, WE TOOK CARE OF A FRIEND'S MONKEY. SHE WAS ALSO FROM INDIA! SHE FELL IN LOVE WITH ME AND THREW THINGS AT YOUR FATHER!

ONCE, WE DROVE ACROSS THE COUNTRY, AND WHEN YOUR BROTHER HAD TO PEE WE HELD HIM OUT THE WINDOW!

ONCE, WE WENT TO A PICNIC AND SOMEONE GAVE ME A STEAK AND WHEN I SAID, "WHICH FAMILY IS THIS FOR?" EVERYONE LAUGHED AND LAUGHED AND LAUGHED.

MY BROTHER HAS SOME THEORIES ON HOW OUR PARENTS' PARENTING SKILLS AFFECTED US.

WE WERE RAISED BY WOLVES. IT'S AMAZING WE SURVIVED AT ALL. EVEN NOW, I JUST LIVE EVERY DAY LIKE KILL OR BE KILLED.

ARUN, YOU'RE A COMPUTER PROGRAMMER.

YEAH, BUT ON THE INSIDE.

EVERY FEW YEARS, MY PARENTS TRIED TO MOVE BACK TO INDIA. EVERY TIME, SOMETHING DIDN'T WORK OUT.

AND THEN WHAT?
AND THEN IT WAS TOO LATE. YOU WERE ALREADY AMERICANS.

CHAPTER 3: SPRING 2015

THAT'S NOT REALLY HOW A KNOCK-KNOCK JOKE WORKS. WATCH.

KNOCK KNOCK.

WHO'S THERE?

CANOE.

CANOE WHO?

CANOE COME OUT AND PLAY WITH ME?

GET IT?

YES!

I JUST THINK IF YOU ASK DADDY HIMSELF, THEN YOU MAKE HIM A PART OF THE CONVERSATION, YOU KNOW? WHICH IS GOOD BECAUSE—

KNOCK KNOCK!

CAN WE— UGH, OKAY, WHO'S THERE?

BIG HEART.

BIG HEART WHO?

BIG HEART UNDERPANTS GORILLA!!!

I AM NOT ASKING DADDY ABOUT IT.
WHY NOT?
BECAUSE I DON'T WANT TO HURT HIS FEELINGS.
BUT IT WON'T HURT HIS FEELINGS!
HE WILL FEEL LEFT OUT.
NO, HE—
BECAUSE WE ARE BROWN AND HE IS NOT AND IT WILL MAKE HIM SAD.
OH.

YOU KNOW WHAT, THOUGH? I DON'T THINK IT WILL. I THINK IF YOU JUST—
KNOCK KNOCK.
—TELL HIM, HE WILL FEEL LIKE HE'S PART OF US, BECAUSE—
KNOCK KNOCK!
—WE'RE A FAMILY AND WE—
KNOCK KNOCK!!!
WHO'S THERE?
CANOE.
CANOE WHO?
CANOE STOP TALKING ABOUT THIS?
HA!!

CHAPTER 4: FAIR & LOVELY

WHEN I WAS FIVE AND WE WENT BACK TO INDIA FOR A VISIT, EVERYONE WAS UPSET ABOUT TWO THINGS. THE FIRST WAS THAT MY BROTHER AND I STILL DID NOT SPEAK MALAYALAM. THE SECOND WAS HOW MUCH I HAD "CHANGED" SINCE I WAS A BABY.
BUT THE MOTHER IS FAIR, NO? AND THE FATHER TOO? EVEN THE BOY IS OKAY.
NOBODY KNOWS WHAT HAPPENED TO THE LITTLE ONE. SO SAD.
I DON'T CHEAT.
WHAT?
THE AUNTIES SAID I'M NOT FAIR, BUT I AM, RIGHT?
OH. DON'T WORRY ABOUT THAT.
BUT I DON'T—
IT'S NOTHING.

AS USUAL, MY BROTHER HAD THE ANSWERS.
IT'S YOUR SKIN COLOR, DOOFUS. "FAIR" MEANS LIGHT-SKINNED.
YOU'RE LIGHT-SKINNED?
I PUT MY ARM NEXT TO HIS. HIS TURNED LIGHTER. IT WAS LIKE MAGIC.
THE NEXT MORNING, I PUT MY ARM NEXT TO MY MOM'S
THAT EVENING, WHEN MY DAD WAS SITTING ON THE VERANDAH, I TRIED TO DO THE SAME THING.
WHAT ARE YOU DOING?
YOU'RE LIGHTER THAN ME, TOO?
ACH! DON'T WORRY ABOUT ALL THAT, MEEMO.
BUT THE AUNTIES SAID—
DON'T LISTEN TO THEM. YOU'RE A PRETTY GIRL.
THAT WAS HOW I LEARNED DARK MEANT UGLY.

TOWARD THE END OF THE VISIT, MY GRANDMOTHER GAVE ME A BOTTLE OF FAIR & LOVELY. I KNEW WHAT IT WAS. I HAD SEEN THE ADVERTISEMENT ON TRAIN STATION WALLS. IT SHOWED A WOMAN'S FACE GETTING LIGHTER AND HAPPIER AND LIGHTER AND HAPPIER.

ABSOLUTELY NOT.

BUT NOW SHE IS BECOMING ONE BLACKIE! AND YOU DON'T STOP IT!

NO!

FOR THE REST OF THE TRIP, EVERY TIME I LOOKED AT MYSELF, I WOULD IMAGINE THE LIGHTER, HAPPIER, PRETTIER ME.

COMING BACK TO NEW MEXICO WAS ALMOST A RELIEF. IN NEW MEXICO, I WASN'T DARK, I WAS JUST BROWN. MY WHOLE FAMILY WAS JUST BROWN. IF PEOPLE NOTICED US, IT WAS BECAUSE WE LOOKED DIFFERENT FROM ALMOST ALL THE OTHER BROWN PEOPLE IN THE STATE, NOT BECAUSE WE LOOKED DIFFERENT FROM EACH OTHER.

IN AMERICA, I WOULD FORGET ABOUT BEING TOO DARK FOR YEARS AT A TIME. THEN I'D MEET NEW INDIANS.
MY SON LOVES TENNIS. VERY INTERESTING FELLOW! BRIGHT FUTURE AHEAD.
HE SOUNDS NICE.
OH, DON'T GET TOO INTERESTED. HE CAN HAVE HIS PICK OF THE LOT!
WHAT?
AND HIS MOTHER WILL ONLY CONSIDER BEAUTIES.
ON VISITS BACK TO INDIA, THE TRAGEDY OF MY SKIN COLOR REMAINED A FAVORITE TOPIC.
THUNGAMUN-GAHUNGABUN-GANAH.
SHE SAYS YOU HAVEN'T GOT GOOD COLOR.
SHE'S DARKER THAN ME!
SO? SHE'S THE COOK.

MY COUSIN EXPLAINED IT TO ME.
IT MAKES YOU SEEM LIKE A SERVANT, SEE? AND THE GOOD BOYS ONLY WANT TO MARRY WHEATISH GIRLS, SO EVERYONE IS JUST FEELING BAD FOR YOUR PARENTS.
MY PARENTS?
BECAUSE IT WILL BE HARD FOR THEM, FINDING SOMEONE WHO WILL SETTLE FOR YOU.
I SWEAR, A GIRL COULD HAVE SEVEN EYES AND LIGHT SKIN AND YOU GUYS WOULD BE LIKE, "SHE'S SUCH A BEAUTY."
NOT TRUE!
COMPARED TO A TOTALLY NORMAL-LOOKING DARK-SKINNED GIRL?
OH, WELL COMPARED TO A DARKIE, SURE.

I COULDN'T STOP THINKING ABOUT IT. I'D BEEN THE WRONG COLOR IN AMERICA MY WHOLE LIFE. BUT IT HURT WORSE SOMEHOW, KNOWING IT WAS THE SAME IN A COUNTRY FULL OF PEOPLE WHO (I HAD THOUGHT) LOOKED LIKE ME.
SO NO ONE IN INDIA WOULD EVER MARRY ME?
WHAT?
I'M TOO DARK FOR ANY SELF-RESPECTING INDIAN GUY AND HIS MOM.
YOU WANT TO MARRY SOMEONE LIKE THAT?
NO! JESUS. I JUST WANT HIM TO WANT TO MARRY ME!
SOUNDS LIKE A BIG PROBLEM.

WELL, I NEVER THOUGHT YOU WERE TOO DARK TO MARRY.
JED.
WHAT?
YOU'RE NOT DOING THAT WHITE GUY THING WHERE YOU PRETEND THAT THIS IS ABOUT YOU BEING ENLIGHTENED INSTEAD OF YOU JUST NEVER CONSIDERING THAT PEOPLE OF COLOR CAN SEE COLOR, TOO, RIGHT?
YUP. NOPE. DEFINITELY WAS NOT DOING THAT AT ALL. EVER. RIGHT.

CHAPTER 5: SUMMER 2015

ALISON IS MY BEST FRIEND. WHEN THINGS GET WEIRD WE GO ON WALKS.
I DON'T KNOW. I DON'T WANT TO, LIKE, FORCE THINGS. BUT I ALSO DON'T WANT Z TO THINK HE CAN'T TALK TO JED ABOUT THIS STUFF, YOU KNOW?
HAS JED TRIED TO TALK TO HIM?
YEAH. CRICKETS.

MEANWHILE, THE STUFF HE ASKS ME...I'VE HAD TO MAKE UP ALL THESE RULES FOR MYSELF! "JUST ANSWER THE QUESTIONS HE ASKS." "DON'T TELL HIM THINGS HE'S NOT READY FOR." BUT WHAT ARE THE RULES WHEN HE ASKS ABOUT THINGS HE'S NOT READY FOR?
ONE WAY
AND IT'S CRAZY BECAUSE HE'S SO ON IT.
NO STOPPING Anytime
YEAH.
WAIT. WHAT?

YOU KNOW, HE JUST PICKS UP ON SO MUCH. IT MUST BE CONFUSING FOR HIM.

YOU THINK I'M CONFUSING HIM?

WHAT?

LIKE, TELLING HIM TOO MUCH?

NO.

I MEAN, I TRY TO KEEP THE NEWS OFF AND HIDE THE NEWSPAPERS AND STUFF. BUT I CAN'T STOP ALL OF IT FROM COMING IN.

YEAH, OF COURSE.

WHAT DO YOU TELL M?
SHE DOESN'T REALLY ASK ABOUT IT YET.
ONE WAY
NO STOPPING Anytime
196 Cold &
I WASN'T SAYING YOU'RE A BAD MOM. YOU KNOW THAT, RIGHT?
I MIGHT BE.
SHE DOESN'T ASK BECAUSE SHE'S FOUR. AND EVEN IF SHE WERE OLDER, SHE'D STILL BE WHITE. IT'S NOT ABOUT MY PARENTING SKILLS.

WHAT IF I'M FUCKING HIM UP?
YOU'RE NOT. YOU'RE TALKING TO HIM LIKE SOMEONE WHO THINKS HIS QUESTIONS ARE IMPORTANT. THAT'S DIFFERENT.
I HOPE SO.

CHAPTER 6: AMERICAN REVOLUTION

MS. MORRELL WAS OUR FIFTH-GRADE TEACHER. SHE WAS THIN AND LOOKED LIKE E.T., ONLY MEAN. SHE WAS MORMON AND EVERYONE IN MY CLASS WAS SCARED OF HER, NOT BECAUSE SHE WAS MORMON, BUT BECAUSE SHE COULD GET MAD ABOUT ANYTHING.
MIRA JACOBS,* IF YOU INSIST ON CHEWING ON YOUR PENCIL LIKE AN ANIMAL THEN I HOPE YOU WILL ALSO INSIST ON STAYING IN THIS CLASSROOM FOR ALL OF LUNCH PERIOD BECAUSE YOU WILL HAVE ALREADY EATEN AND OUR CAFETERIA DOES NOT PERMIT ANIMALS ON THE PREMISES.
*SHE NEVER GOT MY NAME RIGHT. I WAS NEVER NOT SCARED ENOUGH TO TELL HER.

MS. MORRELL HAD RULES.
IF YOU ARE NOT IN YOUR SEAT WHEN THE BELL RINGS THEN YOU ARE LATE, AS FAR AS I AM CONCERNED.
SIT UP STRAIGHT WHEN YOU RAISE YOUR HAND OR I WILL NOT CALL ON YOU.
DO NOT ASK ME IF YOU CAN GO TO THE BATH-ROOM, THAT IS WHAT RECESS IS FOR.
QUIET TIME MEANS I DON'T HEAR A PEEP OUT OF YOU.
YOU ARE ALLOWED TO SHARPEN YOUR PENCIL EXACTLY ONCE A DAY.
TAKE THE LORD'S NAME IN VAIN IN MY CLASSROOM AND YOU WILL MISS RECESS FOR A WEEK. AM I CLEAR?

MS. MORRELL LOVED COLONIAL AMERICANS. SHE SAID THE SETTLERS WERE BRAVER THAN ANY OF US COULD HAVE EVER BEEN, AND WE SHOULD THINK ABOUT THAT THE NEXT TIME WE COMPLAINED ABOUT NOT HAVING A TV IN OUR BEDROOMS. SHE GAVE US ASSIGNMENTS LIKE "MAKE A TOY FROM THE 1800s BUT DO NOT USE ANY MATERIALS OR TOOLS OTHER THAN THOSE AVAILABLE IN THE 1800s AND YES THAT INCLUDES GLUE."
CONGRATULATIONS, MIRA JACOBS. YOUR CORN HUSK DOLL WAS WELL CRAFTED.
REALLY?!?!
CLOSE YOUR MOUTH OR YOU'LL CATCH FLIES.

WE KNEW THE DAUGHTERS OF THE AMERICAN REVOLUTION ESSAY CONTEST WAS A BIG DEAL BECAUSE SHE PRACTICALLY SALUTED AS SHE HANDED OUT EACH FORM.

THE TOPIC THAT YEAR WAS "TOOLS OF EARLY AMERICA." I WROTE ABOUT HAMMERS. A MONTH LATER, MS. MORRELL KEPT ME IN DURING RECESS.

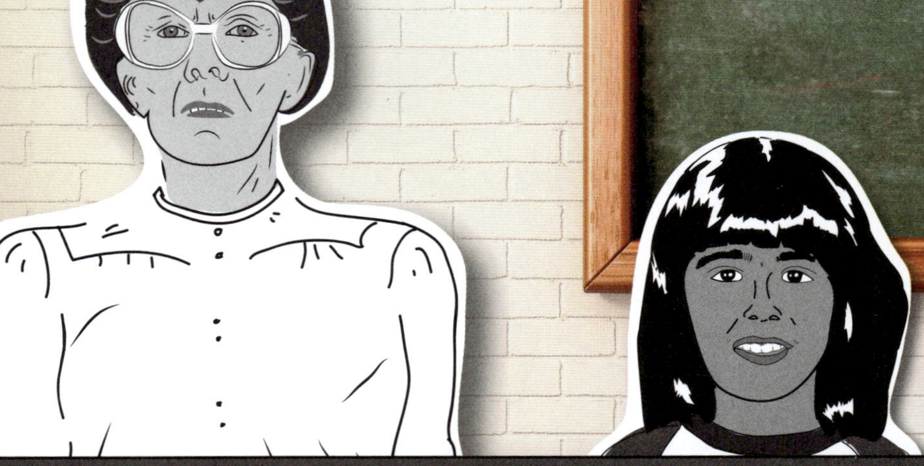

THE DAR RULES SAID I WAS SUPPOSED TO WEAR A DRESS OR A SKIRT AND A BLOUSE AND PANTYHOSE. THE MORNING OF THE LUNCHEON, MY PANTYHOSE KEPT SLIDING DOWN BUT MS. MORRELL DID NOT SEEM UNPLEASED.

YOU WILL NEED TO COMB YOUR HAIR AGAIN BEFORE WE GO.

YES MA'AM.

IT WAS STRANGE IN HER CAR. IN MY HEAD, MS. MORRELL ONLY EXISTED IN FRONT OF A CHALKBOARD OR BEHIND HER DESK. EVERY TIME SHE TURNED THE STEERING WHEEL I THOUGHT SHE MIGHT DISAPPEAR. SHE HAD THE ADDRESS WRITTEN ON A NOTEBOOK ON HER LAP.

DID YOU PRACTICE READING YOUR ESSAY ALOUD LIKE I ASKED?

YES MA'AM.

PRACTICE HADN'T GONE THAT GREAT BUT I WASN'T ABOUT TO TELL MS. MORRELL THAT.
IS THE WHOLE THING ABOUT HAMMERS?
YES! I TOLD YOU IT WAS THE ASSIGNMENT!
BUT SO MANY PAGES?
CAN I PLEASE JUST READ?
SHOULD I LISTEN THE WHOLE TIME?

WHEN WE GOT TO THE ADDRESS, IT DIDN'T LOOK RIGHT.
ABQ CLEANERS House of Quality
HOUSE OF QUALITY ABQ CLEANERS
QUALITY DRY CLEANING COMPLETE LAUNDRY SERVICE
THERE MUST BE A MISTAKE. HOLD ON.
SHE DROVE A FEW BLOCKS DOWN AND PULLED OVER AGAIN. SHE STARED AT THE ADDRESS ON THE PAPER. THEN SHE DROVE US ACROSS THE STREET TO A CONVENIENCE STORE. SHE MADE A PHONE CALL AND THEN ANOTHER AND ANOTHER. SHE CAME BACK TO THE CAR. HER FACE WAS RED. SHE HELD THE STEERING WHEEL SO HARD IT LOOKED LIKE SHE MIGHT BREAK IT. WE SPED OUT OF THE PARKING LOT.
ARE WE GOING BACK TO SCHOOL?
NO. THAT IS ONE THING WE ARE MOST CERTAINLY NOT GOING TO DO, MIRA JACOBS.

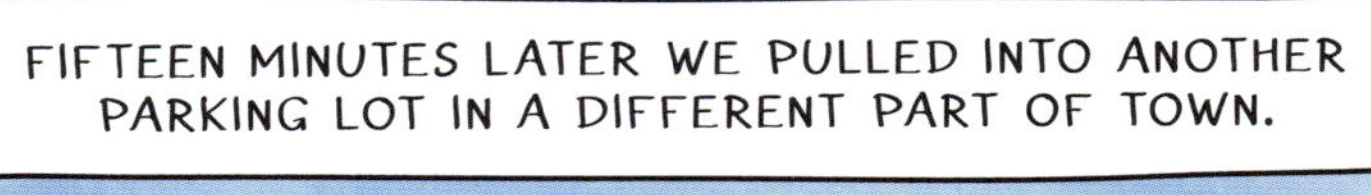
FIFTEEN MINUTES LATER WE PULLED INTO ANOTHER PARKING LOT IN A DIFFERENT PART OF TOWN.
WHERE ARE WE?
THIS IS WHERE THE LUNCHEON IS REALLY BEING HELD.
OH!
I OPENED MY DOOR. MS. MORRELL DID NOT OPEN HERS.
LISTEN, LUNCH MIGHT HAVE STARTED ALREADY.
ARE WE IN TROUBLE?
NO. WE ARE GOING TO GO IN AND YOU ARE GOING TO READ YOUR ESSAY AND YOU'RE GOING TO READ IT WELL, DO YOU UNDERSTAND ME?
YES MA'AM.

IT SMELLED LIKE GRAVY WHEN WE WALKED IN. SOME OF THE WOMEN SAW US AND STOPPED TALKING. I HAD NEVER SEEN SO MANY ADULTS I DIDN'T KNOW. ONE OF THEM STOOD UP AND WALKED TOWARD US.
HI! THERE MUST HAVE BEEN A MIX-UP.
NOT ON OUR END. THIS IS MIRA JACOBS. SHE IS THE FIFTH GRADER WHO WON YOUR ESSAY CONTEST. PERHAPS YOU WOULD LIKE TO HEAR HER ESSAY.
I'M JUST NOT SURE WE HAVE TIME NOW.
SHE HAS PRACTICED FOR THIS.
LET ME SEE WHAT I CAN DO.

I DON'T REMEMBER IF THERE WAS A PODIUM. I DON'T REMEMBER IF I READ MY ESSAY WELL. THE ONLY THING I REMEMBER IS THERE WAS ONE WOMAN WITH BROWN HAIR AND A REALLY NICE SMILE WHO KEPT NODDING ANY TIME I LOOKED UP.
"HAMMERS WERE AMONG THE MOST-USED TOOLS OF THE EARLY AMERICAN SETTLERS."
WHEN I FINISHED, THEY ALL CLAPPED VERY LOUDLY, AND THEN EVERYBODY WAS SMILING. THEY GOT ME A PIECE OF CAKE AND CONGRATULATED ME. MS. MORRELL SAID WE HAD TO GET BACK TO SCHOOL. I FOLLOWED HER OUT OF THE ELKS LODGE AND BACK TO THE CAR.

I PUT ON MY SEATBELT AND WAITED FOR MS. MORRELL TO DRIVE US BACK BUT SHE DIDN'T EVEN START THE CAR.
MIRA JACOBS, I AM GOING TO TELL YOU SOMETHING AND I WANT YOU TO LISTEN CLOSELY.
YOU ARE AN AMERICAN. DO YOU UNDERSTAND ME?
IT SEEMED LIKE A TRICK QUESTION SO I DID NOT ANSWER.

SHE GRABBED MY ARM AND SQUEEZED IT HARD.
YOU ARE AN AMERICAN. I DON'T CARE WHEN YOUR PARENTS CAME HERE. THEY ARE AMERICANS, TOO. DON'T YOU EVER LET ANYONE TELL YOU THAT YOU'RE NOT. DO YOU HEAR ME?
SHE SQUEEZED MY ARM AGAIN. IT SCARED ME. I NODDED.

SHE LET GO OF MY ARM AND STARTED THE CAR.
THAT WAS A VERY GOOD READING. I CAN TELL YOU PRACTICED.
YOU REALLY WANT TO BE A WRITER WHEN YOU GROW UP?
YES MA'AM.
SPEAK UP! NOBODY LIKES A SOFT-TALKER.
YES MA'AM!!
THEN YOU SHOULD.

CHAPTER 7: FALL 2015

KAITLYN AND TANWI ARE ALSO WRITERS. OUR FIRST BOOKS CAME OUT AROUND THE SAME TIME, SO I LEARNED TO LOOK FOR THEIR FACES AMONG THE MOSTLY WHITE ONES AT PUBLISHING EVENTS. THERE'S A PARTICULAR KIND OF CLOSE YOU GET WHEN YOU FIND SOMEONE YOU CAN TRUST IN A SPACE YOU DON'T.
THAT FALL, WE STARTED MEETING OUTSIDE OF WORK EVENTS.
I SWEAR, SOMETIMES I CAN'T TELL IF AMERICA IS GETTING MORE MESSED UP OR IF I'VE JUST RUN OUT OF PATIENCE.
WHY SHOULD WE BE PATIENT? WHERE HAS THAT EVER GOTTEN US?
THIS COUNTRY WAS BUILT ON MESSED UP. IT'S NOT SOME NEW THING.

I KEEP TELLING Z THAT TRUMP ISN'T GOING TO LAST BECAUSE PEOPLE ARE BETTER THAN THIS, BUT THEN—

THEY'RE NOT AND HE GETS EVEN MORE POPULAR! SURPRISE!

I'M JUST SICK OF PEOPLE SAYING WE HAVE TO GIVE HIM A CHANCE, LIKE THE WAY HE'S TALKING ABOUT MEXICANS AND MUSLIMS SOMEHOW DOESN'T COUNT.

WELL, BUT YOU KNOW THOSE MUSLIMS...

GIRL, SHUT UP. YOU KNOW YOU'RE JUST JEALOUS OF US.

IT'S NOT BAD ENOUGH BECAUSE NONE OF IT WILL EVER BE BAD ENOUGH, THOUGH.

I MEAN, THAT'S THE THING, RIGHT? THOSE SAME PEOPLE WHO SAY THEY WILL STOP SUPPORTING HIM IF HE "REALLY DOES SOMETHING" ARE FINE WITH WHAT'S HAPPENING NOW.

SO WHO DOES HE HAVE TO ATTACK BEFORE THEY FINALLY SAY, "OH LOOK, THE RACIST IS RACIST!"

WHITE PEOPLE!

HA.

I'M SERIOUS!

FOR REAL, THOUGH, YOU GUYS. WHAT IS GOING TO FINALLY MAKE THEM SEE HOW BAD HE IS?
NIGHTTIME RAIDS ON IMMIGRANT FAMILIES!
BANNING MUSLIMS!!
PRISON CAMPS!!
NAZI PARADES!!!

I'M SCARED.

CHAPTER 8: OUR BODIES, OURSELVES

IN SIXTH GRADE, SOME OF THE KIDS IN MY CLASS STARTED "GOING OUT," WHICH MEANT THAT YOU SAT AT THE SAME TABLE AT LUNCH AND MIGHT EVEN KISS SOMETIMES AT A BIRTHDAY PARTY OR MAYBE A SCHOOL DANCE.
YOU SHOULD GO OUT WITH TONY.
BUT I DON'T LIKE TONY.
BUT YOU MATCH. AND NONE OF THE OTHER BOYS WANT TO KISS YOU. WE'VE ASKED.

SLUMBER PARTIES WERE REALLY JUST AN EXCUSE TO TRY OUT EVERYTHING WE WERE READING IN JUDY BLUME BOOKS.
I FEEL LIKE WE SHOULD PRACTICE WITH TONGUE. JUST SO WE'RE, LIKE, BETTER AT IT. FOR BOYS.
GOOD IDEA.

IN HIGH SCHOOL, I KNEW YOU WERE SUPPOSED TO BE IN LOVE TO HOOK UP SO YOU WEREN'T A SLUT. BUT FALLING IN LOVE WAS HARD.
I DON'T KNOW IF IT'S THE WHOLE INDIAN THING OR WHAT, BUT SOMETIMES IT FEELS LIKE YOU CAN READ MY MIND.
HUH.
WAIT. ARE YOU READING MY MIND RIGHT NOW?
NO.
EVEN WHEN YOU WERE IN LOVE, IT COULD GET WEIRD. 
DO YOU THINK YOU TASTE DIFFERENT THAN OTHER GIRLS?
I DON'T THINK SO.
WAIT. I TASTE DIFFERENT THAN OTHER GIRLS?
HARD TO TELL.

THE MOST COMFORTABLE I EVER FELT WAS WHEN I COULD BE WITH SOMEONE I DIDN'T KNOW AND WOULD PROBABLY NEVER SEE AGAIN.

WHAT'S YOUR NAME?

MIRA.

WANT TO GO DRINK IN THE ARROYO?

SURE.

CHAPTER 9: PERFECT TOGETHER

C WAS MY FIRST REAL BOYFRIEND. HE WAS A JUNIOR WHEN I WAS A FRESHMAN, A SAXOPHONE PRODIGY, AND THE STAR OF THE SOCCER TEAM. WHENEVER HE TALKED TO ME, I FELT LIKE I WAS WATCHING A MOVIE OF MY OWN LIFE.
YOU NEED A RIDE HOME?
IT'S FAR.
FAR IS GOOD.
Kroger

I LIKED BEING C'S GIRLFRIEND. I LIKED SITTING IN HIS CAR AND LISTENING TO PRINCE AT NIGHT. I LIKED THE WAY HE MADE ME FEEL LIKE SOMETHING BRIGHT AND RARE AND PRECIOUS.
YOU'RE BEAUTIFUL.
NO.
WHAT?
I MEAN THANKS. THANK YOU. FOR SAYING SO.
CALM DOWN.

HE KNEW THINGS ABOUT OUR HIGH SCHOOL THAT I DIDN'T, LIKE HOW ALL THE TEACHERS WERE WATCHING HIM EXTRA HARD BUT WOULD NEVER ACTUALLY REPRIMAND HIM BECAUSE THEY WERE TOO SCARED.

ALL THAT DIVERSITY TALK IS JUST THEIR WAY OF SAYING "DON'T ASK ME TO THINK ABOUT HOW I REALLY FEEL ABOUT YOU."

HE SAID THE KIDS IN SCHOOL IDOLIZED HIM BUT DIDN'T KNOW HIM.

THEY JUST WANT TO SAY THEY HAVE A BLACK FRIEND.

COME ON. THEY LIKE YOU!

IT'S NOT ABOUT THEM LIKING ME, MIRA. GOD, IS THAT ALL YOU THINK ABOUT?

NO!*

* YES.

ONE DAY HE HEARD SOME SENIOR GIRLS TALKING TO ME IN THE HALL.

YOU GUYS LOOK LIKE SERIOUSLY PERFECT TOGETHER.

THANKS!

WHY DO YOU LET THEM SAY THAT SHIT TO YOU?

WHAT?
WHY DO YOU LET THEM TELL YOU WE BELONG TOGETHER BECAUSE WE'RE NOT WHITE?
THAT'S NOT WHAT THEY WERE SAYING!
OF COURSE THAT IS WHAT THEY WERE SAYING! WHAT ELSE WERE THEY SAYING?
BUT WE DO LOOK GOOD TOGETHER!
FUCK, MAN.

HOMECOMING WAS A BIG DEAL. I WASN'T ALLOWED TO GO ALONE WITH A BOY SO C AND I WENT WITH MY FRIEND AND A FRIEND OF HIS I'D NEVER MET BEFORE.
IT'S LIKE WE'RE A BENETTON AD.
TOTALLY.
J HAD A NICE SMILE AND WORE A DARK BLUE SUIT INSTEAD OF A TUX.
MIRA, YOUR FOLKS ARE INDIAN FROM INDIA?
YEAH.
HOW DID THEY END UP HERE?
MY DAD DID HIS RESIDENCY HERE. HE'S A DOCTOR.
OH YEAH? WHAT KIND?
HE'S A CARDIOVAS-CULAR SURGEON.
HUH.

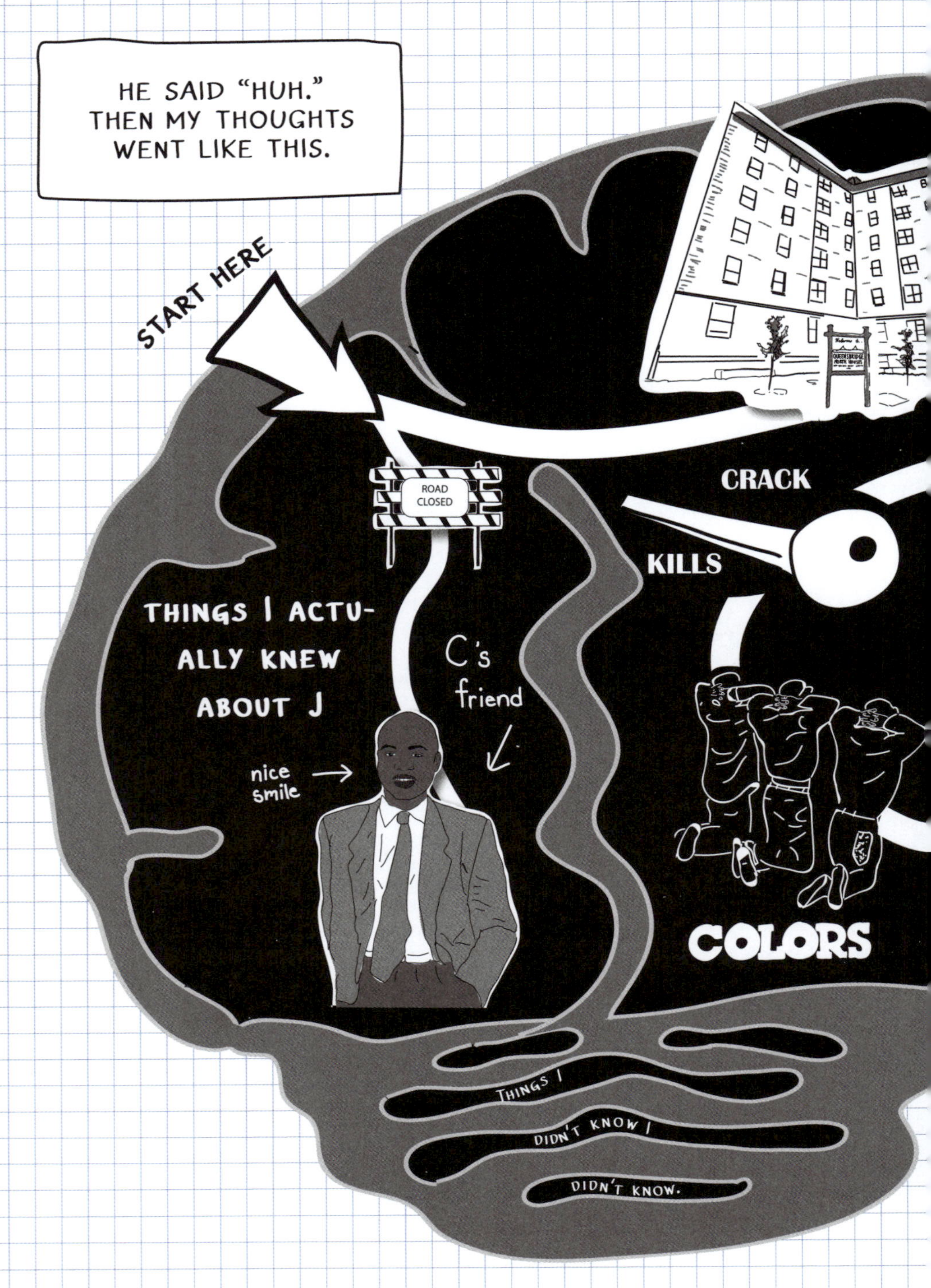
HE SAID "HUH."
THEN MY THOUGHTS
WENT LIKE THIS.
START HERE
ROAD
CLOSED
CRACK
KILLS
THINGS I ACTU-
ALLY KNEW
ABOUT J
C's
friend
nice
smile
COLORS
THINGS I
DIDN'T KNOW I
DIDN'T KNOW.

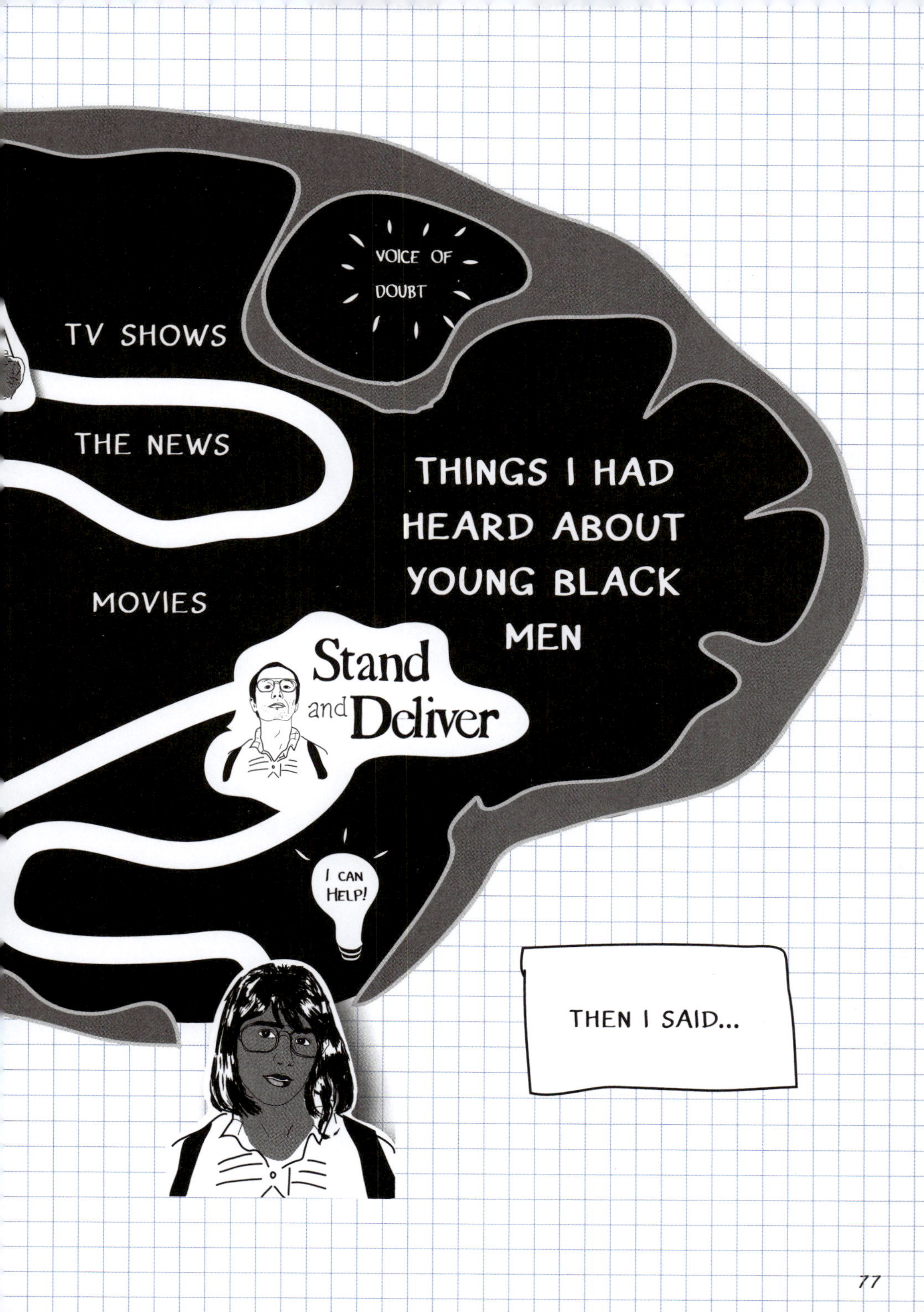
VOICE OF DOUBT
TV SHOWS
THE NEWS
MOVIES
THINGS I HAD HEARD ABOUT YOUNG BLACK MEN
Stand and Deliver
I CAN HELP!
THEN I SAID...

THAT MEANS HEART DOCTOR.
NO ONE SAID ANYTHING. I LOOKED IN THE REARVIEW MIRROR. NO ONE WOULD LOOK AT ME. C SHOOK HIS HEAD.
I JUST MEANT—
NO.
J, I DIDN'T MEAN—
WHATEVER.

WE WENT TO THE DANCE. WE WENT TO THE PARTIES AFTERWARD. WE DRANK BEER AND KISSED. BUT LATER THAT NIGHT, WHEN WE WERE FINALLY ALONE, IT WAS WEIRD.

ARE YOU MAD AT ME?

NO.

THEN WHAT'S WRONG?

NOTHING.

THAT'S NOT TRUE. TELL ME.

JUST FORGET IT, OKAY?

BUT I COULDN'T FORGET IT. NEITHER COULD HE.

CHAPTER 10: WINTER 2015

IT'S MORE LIKE WHEN ONE RACE OF PEOPLE GETS AHEAD BY KEEPING ANOTHER DOWN WITH A WHOLE SYSTEM. SO I WOULDN'T REALLY CALL A BLACK OR BROWN PERSON IN AMERICA RACIST, BECAUSE WE DON'T HAVE THE SYSTEM. BUT, LIKE, ANYONE OF ANY COLOR CAN BE A MEAN JERK.
MOMMY!
SORRY, BAD WORD. I JUST MEANT THAT ANYONE CAN MAKE SOMEONE FEEL BAD JUST BECAUSE THEY DON'T LIKE THAT PERSON'S RACE. AND THAT'S YUCKY. BUT IT'S NOT ALWAYS RACIST. MAKE SENSE?
NO.
SO, LIKE, LET'S SAY YOU COULD BE MEAN TO SOMEONE AND IT WOULD HURT THEIR FEELINGS, OR YOU COULD BE MEAN TO SOMEONE AND IT WOULD MAKE IT HARD FOR THEM TO GO TO SCHOOL, OR GET A JOB OR STAY OUT OF JAIL. THOSE ARE PRETTY DIFFERENT KINDS OF MEAN, RIGHT?
IF SOMEONE MADE ME NOT BE ABLE TO GO TO SCHOOL, COULD I HAVE MORE TV TIME?
中華髮型屋
CHUNG WAH BEAUTY SALON
PELL ST.

OKAY, LOOK: RACISM IS ABOUT USING POWER TO KEEP OTHER PEOPLE DOWN.
LIKE IRON MAN!
HUH?
BECAUSE NO ONE REALLY KNOWS WHAT COLOR IRON MAN IS WHEN HE'S WEARING HIS SUIT BECAUSE THEN HE IS RED WITH GOLD.
UM...
BUT UNDER HIS SUIT, IRON MAN IS WHITE! SO HE COULD BE RACIST!
WHAT?
BUT NOT THE FALCON. THE FALCON COULD NOT BE RACIST.
I KNEW YOU WERE TOO YOUNG FOR THOSE MOVIES.

THERE ARE NO BROWN SUPERHEROES.
REALLY? STILL?
NOT IN *CAPTAIN AMERICA: THE WINTER SOLDIER*. LIKE INDIAN GUY. WHERE IS INDIAN GUY?
THE ETERNAL QUESTION.
IF THERE WAS INDIAN GUY, COULD HE BE RACIST?
WAIT, WHAT? WHY WOULD YOU WANT HIM TO BE—
I DON'T WANT HIM TO BE, BUT COULD HE BE? AGAINST THE FALCON?
OH.
UH.
HUH.

I GUESS I STILL WOULDN'T CALL IT RACIST BECAUSE OF THE WHOLE SYSTEM THING. BUT SOME INDIANS CAN BE REALLY...MEAN TO PEOPLE IN OTHER RACES.
MEAN?
WELL, KINDA LIKE, THINKING WE'RE BETTER THAN THEM BECAUSE WE'VE BEEN SUCCESSFUL IN AMERICA.
BUT THAT'S RACIST!
YEAH. I MEAN, NO, IT'S CALLED BIGOTRY BUT BASICALLY, YEAH.

YOU OKAY?
I THOUGHT WE WERE THE GOOD GUYS.
OH.
I GUESS WE'RE BOTH, RIGHT? WE'RE IN THE MIDDLE PLACE WHERE SOMETIMES WE GET TREATED BADLY AND SOMETIMES WE DO IT TO OTHER PEOPLE. BUT I MEAN, THAT'S NOT THE END OF THE WORLD, RIGHT? KNOWING WE'VE GOT ROOM FOR IMPROVEMENT?
I'D RATHER JUST BE THE GOOD GUYS.
JOE'S SHANGHAI
鹿鳴春
中華國貨參茸
川外
錦江飯店
13 PELL ST

CHAPTER 11: AND THEN IT GOT A LITTLE WEIRD

COLLEGE WAS GREAT. IT MEANT MEETING WAY MORE PEOPLE I COULD ACTUALLY CONNECT WITH.

LAST NIGHT WAS COOL. I LIKED YOUR FRIENDS.

YEAH. I THINK I'M NOT ATTRACTED TO YOU.

WHAT?

I JUST THOUGHT YOU, I DON'T KNOW, TALKED LESS.

YOU AREN'T ATTRACTED TO ME?

I FUCKING LOVE YOUR SKIN.

I FUCKING LOVE YOUR EVERYTHING.

WAIT, IS THAT RACIST?

I DON'T KNOW.

OH MY GOD. DOES THIS MEAN WE'RE LESBIANS NOW? DO WE HAVE TO GO, LIKE, MARCH AND SHIT?
BECAUSE I'VE GOT ENOUGH ON MY PLATE.
I DON'T KNOW WHY IT'S SUCH A BIG DEAL FOR SOME PEOPLE. WHAT COLOR SOMEONE IS MAKES NO DIFFERENCE TO ME.
WELL YEAH, BUT YOU'RE WHITE.
SO?

MY GIRLFRIEND IS GOING TO LOVE YOU.
WHAT?
SHE'S INDIAN, TOO!
WHAT?!
WHY IS IT ALWAYS GOOD WITH US? 
STOP. YOU'RE GOING TO JINX IT.
I'M NOT GOING TO GODDAMN JINX IT!*

* JINXED IT.

CHAPTER 12: I'M NOT NERVOUS, YOU ARE

I JUST MEAN, I DIDN'T KNOW A LOT BEFORE. I GREW UP IN A SMALL TOWN, SO WE NEVER, LIKE, TALKED ABOUT IT OPENLY OR WHATEVER.
BUT I'VE MET SO MANY NOW! AND THEY'RE REALLY NICE, YOU KNOW?
JESUS CHRIST. LESBIANS ARE LIKE EVERYONE FUCKING ELSE, WE JUST FUCK WOMEN.
YES. RIGHT. OF COURSE.*
* LONGEST, QUIETEST RIDE TO ANYWHERE EVER

CHAPTER 13: AMERICAN LOVE

FINE. SO WHAT'S AMERICAN LOVE?
PASSION! SCANDAL! AFFAIRS! SLINKY OUTFITS! ELIZABETH TAYLOR! *DALLAS!* THE MORGANS! THE PARKERS! THE LEES!
NOW YOU'RE JUST SHOUTING OUT NAMES OF FRIENDS WHO GOT DIVORCED.
THE McLAUGHLINS! THE WILSONS!

MY PARENTS HAD THEORIES ON SUCCESSFUL MARRIAGES.
THE PROBLEM WITH THESE AMERICANS IS THEY ARE ALWAYS SAYING, "YOU'RE NOT WHO I MARRIED," AND GETTING DIVORCED.
INDIANS NEVER DO THAT. WHY NOT?
BECAUSE WE NEVER KNEW EACH OTHER IN THE FIRST PLACE!
LOTS OF THEORIES...
WHEN YOU HAVE MORE IN COMMON, YOU HAVE LESS TO WORRY ABOUT.
NOT THAT WHO YOU MARRY IS UP TO US.
NO! YOU DO WHAT YOU WANT. NONE OF OUR BUSINESS!
I'M SURE THE MIXED MARRIAGES CAN WORK TOO, SOMETIMES.
BUT IT'S HARD, I THINK, FOR THE KIDS.

BY MY EARLY 20s, ALL OF THIS LIVED IN A PRETTY STRANGE PLACE IN MY HEAD.

A FRIEND OF YOUR GREAT-AUNT'S SON, HE LOVES LONG NIGHTS INDOORS, WEEKENDS AT YOUR PARENTS' HOUSE, AND STAYING MARRIED NO MATTER WHAT! SAY HELLO TO BACHELOR #1!
LOOKING TO BLEND SEAMLESSLY INTO AMERICA WHILE FEELING MORE ALONE THAN EVER IN YOUR SOUL? HERE'S BACHELOR #2!
BORN THERE BUT RAISED HERE, THIS YOUNG MAN COMES WITH JUST ENOUGH FRICTION TO KEEP THINGS INTERESTING, UNDERSTANDS PARTS OF YOU THAT YOU THOUGHT NO ONE EVER WOULD, AND IS RUMORED TO EXIST! BACHELOR #3, ARE YOU THERE?

LUCKILY, MY BROTHER HAD ALL THE SAME ISSUES I DID, WAS EQUALLY COMMITTED TO POOR DATING CHOICES, AND LIVED 15 MINUTES AWAY FROM ME IN SEATTLE. ONE OF US WAS ALWAYS BREAKING UP WITH SOMEONE OR GETTING BROKEN UP WITH BY SOMEONE.

MY BROTHER HAD A TYPE: BLOND, ATHLETIC, WRONG FOR HIM. I MOSTLY REMEMBERED THEM BY THEIR UNDOINGS.

THE ONE WHO DIDN'T LIKE HIS FRIENDS

THE ONE WHO WAS COMPETITIVE ABOUT EVERYTHING

HE TURNED MY EXES INTO COUNTRY WESTERN SONG TITLES.

HE SAID I WOULD UNDERSTAND IF I WERE A REAL WRITER.

"MOPEY POET, WHY'D YA BLOW IT?"

HE TOLD ME BEER FOR BREAKFAST IS NORMAL!

"HE COULDA BEEN YOUR LOVER IF HE WOULDA HAD A LIVER."

THE GOOD PART ABOUT COMMUNAL SIBLING HEART-ACHE IS THAT YOU GET A CERTAIN KIND OF CLARITY.

IT'S JUST THAT WE'RE TOO KIND AND MATURE FOR EVERYONE AND WE NEED TO WAIT UNTIL THEY CATCH UP TO THE VERY HIGH LEVEL WE'RE OPERATING AT.

SHOULD WE FILL THE PAIN WITH PIZZA?

YES.

SCORPIONS

AND EVEN WHEN THAT CLARITY WEARS OFF, YOU STILL HAVE YOUR SIBLING.

IT'S OUR PARENTS' FAULT. DO YOU THINK THEY EVEN LOVE EACH OTHER?

WHY WOULD YOU EVER MAKE ME THINK ABOUT THAT?

SO WHEN ARUN BECAME REALLY EXCITED ABOUT A NEW WOMAN AFTER HANGING OUT A FEW TIMES, IT FELT DIFFERENT.

I THOUGHT IT WOULDN'T WORK OUT. MAYBE IT WOULD GO AWRY OUT OF THE BLUE, LIKE IT DID WITH THE ONE WHO SUDDENLY WENT BACK TO DATING WOMEN. BUT THEN I MET LOPA AND SAW HOW THEY SHARED SOME DEEP CORE VALUES.

1.
WERE EQUALLY CHILL ABOUT TRADITION
NOVEMBER
DIWALI
Thanksgiving
2.
BELIEVED DOGS ARE BETTER THAN HUMANS
3.
TREATED PARENTS LIKE WELL-MEANING INTERLOPERS FROM ANOTHER PLANET

AT THE WEDDING MY PARENTS WANDERED AROUND LIKE LOST CHILDREN FROM A FAIRY TALE WHOSE HOME HAD COME AND FOUND THEM.
HE LOOKS SO HAPPY.
IT'S SO WONDERFUL! I CAN'T BELIEVE IT!

AND WHAT ABOUT YOU, MIRA? YOU'VE MET SOMEBODY?
NOPE.
DON'T WAIT TOO LONG! NOTHING GOOD COMES OF IT.
YUP.

WE THINK OUR HEARTS BREAK ONLY FROM ENDINGS—THE LOVE GONE, THE ROOMS EMPTY, THE FUTURE UNHAPPENING AS WE STAND READY TO STEP INTO IT—BUT WHAT ABOUT HOW THEY CAN SHATTER IN THE FACE OF WHAT IS POSSIBLE?

CHAPTER 14: WELCOME TO THE BIG CITY

I MOVED FROM SEATTLE TO NEW YORK TO BE A WRITER IN 1997. I TEMPED DURING THE DAYS AND TOOK ODD JOBS ON NIGHTS AND WEEKENDS. ONCE, SOMEONE KNEW SOMEONE WHO HIRED FACT CHECKERS AT *VANITY FAIR*.

WE PAY $300 A WEEK TO START.

OH. I THOUGHT IT WAS FULL-TIME.

IT IS.

BUT WHO COULD POSSIBLY LIVE ON THAT?!?!?*

*LONGEST PAUSE KNOWN TO NEW YORK MAGAZINE INDUSTRY

THE DAYS I COULDN'T GET WORK, I WOULD WALK AROUND THE CITY AND TRY NOT TO PANIC ABOUT MY BANK ACCOUNT, OR THE JOBS I DIDN'T HEAR ABOUT, OR THE JOBS I DID HEAR ABOUT BUT KNEW I'D NEVER BE CONSIDERED FOR, OR THE THINGS PEOPLE TOLD ME ONCE THEY KNEW I WANTED TO BE A WRITER.

IT'S AN UNPAID INTERNSHIP. WE ALL PAY OUR DUES.

THE WEB HAS LOWER STANDARDS. MAYBE START THERE.

SHE USED TO BE AN EDITOR BUT SHE'S LOOKING FOR A NANNY. YOU WANT TO CONNECT?

ETHNIC SELLS.

3,000 WORDS. NO PAY BUT GREAT EXPOSURE.

NO SERIOUS WRITER WOULD WRITE FOR THE WEB.

GOD, IF *YOU* CAN'T GET A JOB WITH THE WHOLE DIVERSITY THING, THE REST OF US ARE FUCKED.

DO NOT TAKE AN INTERNSHIP. THEY WILL NEVER STOP SEEING YOU AS THE INTERN.

TOO BAD WE'VE ALREADY HAD OUR INDIAN LIT MOMENT!

HE'S AN EDITOR. HE'S LOOKING FOR AN ASSISTANT. I HEARD HE LIKES DARK GIRLS. YOUR CALL.

DON'T GHETTOIZE YOURSELF WITH ETHNIC WRITING.

CHAPTER 15: SPRING 2016

HIS IDEAS ARE SMALL. HIS ATTENTION SPAN IS SMALL. AND THIS THING ABOUT MUSLIMS IS DISGUSTING, ESPECIALLY IF YOU'RE JEWISH.
I'M JEWISH!
EXACTLY. AND DO YOU KNOW WHAT HAPPENED TO THE JEWS DURING WORLD WAR II? AMERICANS THOUGHT THEY WERE NAZI SPIES AND WOULDN'T LET THEM IN THE COUNTRY.
DR. JAY'S
BANANA REPUBLIC
FACTORY STORE
THEY WERE SPIES?
NO, THEY WEREN'T. IT WAS THIS WHOLE...THING...A LIE, BASICALLY. AND OUR GOVERNMENT REPEATED IT SO WE WOULDN'T HAVE TO FEEL BAD ABOUT TURNING JEWS AWAY.
DR. JAY'
MENS
BUT THEN WHERE DID THEY GO?
TO THE CAMPS. AND LOT OF THEM DIED THERE.
OH NO!
JED!

OKAY, OKAY, MOMMY IS GIVING ME A LOOK. THE POINT IS, AMERICA IS A COUNTRY OF IMMIGRANTS. A LOT OF PEOPLE COME FROM REALLY TOUGH SITUATIONS, SCARY SITUATIONS, SITUATIONS THAT NO ONE SHOULD BE IN. AND JEWS, ESPECIALLY, HAVE TO PAY ATTENTION TO THIS. OUR WHOLE HISTORY IS OF BEING DRIVEN OUT OF PLACES. IF WE DON'T TURN AND HELP PEOPLE WHO ARE HAVING THE SAME THING HAPPEN TO THEM, WE ARE NO BETTER THAN THE ONES WHO DID IT TO US, SO—
BLACK PEOPLE?
WHAT?
CAME HERE TO GET AWAY FROM BAD THINGS IN THEIR SITUATIONS?
OH. NO. NO, THAT IS A GOOD POINT, BUT WHAT I MEANT WAS—
NATIVE AMERICANS?

WHO ARE GRANDMA AND GRANDPA VOTING FOR?
I'LL TELL YOU WHO THEY AREN'T VOTING FOR, EVER: HILLARY CLINTON.
WHY NOT?
THEY'RE NOT FANS.
WHAT IF IT'S HILLARY CLINTON VERSUS DONALD TRUMP?
THAT'S NOT GOING TO HAPPEN.
HOW DO YOU KNOW?
JUST...BECAUSE.
DO NOT ENTER
EPT BUSES &
S WITH PERMIT

LOOK, DADDY AND I GREW UP WITH A LOT OF REPUBLICANS. THEY CARE ABOUT THIS COUNTRY TOO MUCH TO VOTE FOR DONALD TRUMP.
GOOD GOD. COMING DOWN ON AN ESCALATOR TO ANNOUNCE YOUR PRESIDENCY IN FRONT OF ACTORS YOU HIRED TO CLAP??? WHO DOES THAT?! WHAT A SHAM.
WOULD HE PAY ME TO CLAP FOR HIM?
YOU'RE NOT CLAP-PING FOR THAT MAN!
I MEAN, EVERYONE WHO'S ACTUALLY WORKED WITH HIM KNOWS. THE EMPEROR HAS NO CLOTHES!
WHO IS THE EMPEROR?
TRUMP!

CHAPTER 16: LOVE MARRIAGE

WHEN I WAS GROWING UP, MY PARENTS DID NOT HUG. THEY DID NOT KISS. THEY DID NOT EVEN GO TO PARTIES IN THE SAME CAR.

ARE YOU GOING TO THE KOSHYS' TONIGHT?

YOU GO. I'LL MEET YOU IF I CAN.

THE KIDS AND I WILL BE THERE UNTIL NINE.

COMPARED TO SOME OF MY FRIENDS, I HAD NOTHING TO COMPLAIN ABOUT...

I HEARD MY MOM TELL MY AUNT SHE WANTS A DIVORCE.

MY DAD ISN'T LIVING WITH US UNTIL HE CAN GET HIS ACT TOGETHER.

MINE JUST GOT MARRIED FOR THE THIRD TIME. LIKE THAT'S GONNA WORK OUT.

MY PARENTS DRIVE SEPA-RATE CARS EVERYWHERE.

...BUT I KNEW THERE WAS SOMETHING SIMILARLY SAD UNDERNEATH IT ALL.

May 5, 1984

Other people's parents:	My parents:
· fall in love	· didn't fall in love
· fall out of love	· couldn't fall out of love
· get divorced	· stay married
· seem lonely	· seem lonely

BY COLLEGE, I GOT USED TO IT.
YOU WANT TO GO TO A MOVIE WITH US?
YOU GO. I'LL MEET YOU AFTER IF I GET DONE WITH ROUNDS.
OKAY!

IT WAS ABOUT THAT TIME THAT I REALIZED SPACE COULD BE NICE IN A RELATIONSHIP.

I THOUGHT WE COULD MAYBE GO SEE THAT BAND AT THE LAKESIDE AND THEN SEE *THE TRUMAN SHOW* AND THEN DO OUR LAUNDRY AND THEN GET BRUNCH ON SUNDAY OR SOMETHING?

THE FIRST TIME I SAW MY PARENTS HOLDING HANDS WAS AT MY BROTHER'S WEDDING. I THOUGHT MAYBE THEY JUST GOT NERVOUS.

BUT A YEAR LATER, I WENT HOME FOR A VISIT AND SAW MY PARENTS DOING MANY NEW THINGS.

1.

SITTING ABNORMALLY CLOSE TO EACH OTHER AT THE KITCHEN TABLE

So?

2.

GOING PLACES IN THE SAME CAR

3.

GIGGLING IN THE MIDDLE OF THE NIGHT

AND WHATEVER THAT WAS IN THE KITCHEN...

THAT NEXT DAY, I CALLED MY BROTHER IN A PANIC.

IT'S LIKE THEY'VE...**FALLEN IN LOVE?** I MEAN, THE OTHER DAY, I THINK I SAW...

WHAT?

THEY WERE KISSING BY THE FRIDGE.

WHAT? DON'T TELL ME THIS STUFF!

YOU ASKED!

YEAH, BUT I DON'T WANT TO KNOW.

OH MY GOD. IT'S GOING TO BE ALL OF YOU.

ALL OF US WHAT?

YOU'LL BE TEAM LOVE MARRIAGE. AND EVERYONE WILL THINK I'M SOME BLACK-SHEEP LONE-REJECT JEALOUS WEIRDO, AND I WILL BE.

I THINK YOU'RE HAVING A SEIZURE.

THE DAY BEFORE I LEFT TO GO BACK TO NEW YORK, I FINALLY SNAPPED.
OKAY, WHAT IS HAPPENING WITH YOU GUYS?
WHO?
YOU AND DAD! YOU ARE ACTING WEIRDER THAN NORMAL.
WEIRD HOW?
I DON'T KNOW! HOLDING HANDS?
WHEN DID WE HOLD HANDS?
MONTHS AGO!
PHILLIP, MIRA IS UPSET BECAUSE WE HELD HANDS MONTHS AGO.
QUICK! GIVE ME YOUR HAND! LET'S MAKE HER UPSET NOW!

HOW HAD MY ARRANGED-MARRIAGE PARENTS FALLEN INTO A LOVE MARRIAGE? WHAT WAS NEXT, AMERICAN LOVE? BACK IN NEW YORK, IT WAS HARD TO EXPLAIN WHY IT MADE ME SO NERVOUS.

I DON'T KNOW. I WOULDN'T MIND HAVING MY PARENTS FALL IN LOVE.

YOU DON'T UNDERSTAND. THEY DON'T DO FALLING IN LOVE. IT'S LIKE GENETIC OR SOMETHING.

IF YOU SAY SO.

BUT I KNEW WHAT I WAS REALLY WORRIED ABOUT.

Team Love Marriage
· Mom
· Dad
· Arun

Team Alone
· Me

CHAPTER 17: BIG CITY ROMANCE

THE GREAT THING ABOUT NEW YORK IS THAT IT'S VERY SOPHISTICATED.

HOW COME IF YOU DATE WHITE GUYS IT ISN'T A FETISH, BUT IF I'M INTO INDIAN WOMEN IT'S SOME *THING*?

I THINK—

I MEAN, IT'S NOT LIKE I'M HURTING ANYONE, RIGHT?

I—

SO I HAPPEN TO THINK INDIAN WOMEN ARE UNBELIEVABLY HOT! SO SUE ME!

"BISEXUAL" IS JUST ANOTHER WORD FOR "SCARED OF YOURSELF."

BUT I DON'T FEEL SCARED OF—

CALL ME WHEN YOU'VE FIGURED IT OUT.

KAMA SUTRA?

WHAT?

IT'S A BOOK OF SEX SPELLS.
HOW DO YOU NOT KNOW THAT?

STOP.

I CAN LEND YOU MINE
IF YOU'RE INTERESTED.

NO, REALLY.

WHAT ARE
YOU DOING?

WHAT YOU WERE
HOPING FOR?

CHAPTER 18: SUMMER 2016

AFTER TRUMP WON THE PRIMARIES, EVERYONE HAD A THEORY.

HE'S NOT EVEN REALLY RACIST—THAT'S JUST WHAT HE'S USING TO APPEAL TO HIS BASE.

OH FOR SURE.

YOUR CHEETO JESUS ISN'T GOING TO SAVE YOU!

I MEAN, THIS IS JUST A LAST GASP OF A DYING, ANGRY BREED. GET OVER IT, FELLAS.

YOU KNOW HE ONLY WON BECAUSE THE LEFT PLAYED RIGHT INTO HIS HANDS WITH THIS IDENTITY POLITICS CRAP!

TELL ME ABOUT IT.

CHAPTER 19: THE NEUROPSYCHOLOGIST

I WAS LIVING IN WILLIAMSBURG, WHERE THE RENTS WERE STILL LOW AND YOU COULD SEE ALL OF GLITTERING MANHATTAN IF YOU WALKED DOWN TO THE EAST RIVER. NOBODY WALKED DOWN TO THE EAST RIVER.

COLUMBIA IS, LIKE, SUPER FAR AWAY, DAD.

NO HARM IN JUST MEETING. IT'S NOT LIKE YOU HAVE TO MAKE SOME BIG DECISION.

I DON'T KNOW.

HE'S A NICE KID.

SAYS HIS DAD.

AND IT'S NOT LIKE YOU'VE BEEN DOING SO WELL ON YOUR OWN.

MY DAD WAS RIGHT. MONTHS EARLIER, IN A FIT OF CLARITY, I HAD BROKEN UP WITH A NICE BUT WRONG-FOR-ME BOYFRIEND. NOTHING HAD BEEN PARTICULARLY CLEAR SINCE.
MOM AND I HAVE BEEN WORRIED. YOU SEEM STRANGE LATELY.
BECAUSE BREAKING UP WITH NICE PEOPLE MAKES YOU STRANGE!
AND YOU SHOULD HAVE CHILDREN BEFORE IT'S TOO LATE.
I THINK IT'S A GREAT IDEA!
JESUS, MOM. HOW LONG HAVE YOU BEEN THERE?
HE'S A NEUROPSYCHOLOGIST, HE'S YOUR AGE, AND HE GREW UP IN AMERICA! YOU TWO WILL HAVE SO MANY THINGS IN COMMON!
THE NEUROPSYCHOLOGY ALONE.

I TOLD THEM I WOULD THINK ABOUT IT. I WALKED AROUND WILLIAMSBURG TRYING NOT TO THINK ABOUT IT.

WHEN I GOT HOME, THERE WAS AN EMAIL FROM MY FAVORITE GREAT-AUNT IN INDIA.

My Dear Mira,

Why is it that all of our best and brightest run off to America and marry these American nobodies? And what kind of country is it where children listen to other children about who to spend the rest of their lives with but never their parents? You've always been such a bright thing. Surely you're smarter?

Sara Kochamma

Dear Sara Kochamma,

Nice try. I am not doing it. You are still my favorite kochamma, though.

Love,
Mira

THE NEXT DAY, MY GREAT-UNCLE, BEDRIDDEN WITH CANCER, CALLED.

MIRA, MOL, LISTEN, JUST MEET WITH HIM. JUST ONE TIME. IT'S A SMALL-SMALL THING TO DO FOR ALL OF US WHO WANT TO SEE YOU HAPPY. PLEASE.

CAN'T I JUST DO SOME OTHER SMALL-SMALL THING FOR YOU?

AND THEN I WILL KNOW THAT YOU ARE TAKEN CARE OF BEFORE I GO.

CHRIST.

I CAN'T HEAR. YOU SAID YES?

I TOLD MYSELF I WAS DOING IT BECAUSE OF THE BREAKUP. AND FOR MY GREAT-UNCLE. AND BECAUSE MY BROTHER HAD FALLEN IN LOVE WITH AN INDIAN WOMAN. AND BECAUSE MY PARENTS HAD FALLEN IN LOVE WITH EACH OTHER. BUT REALLY, IT WAS SIMPLER THAN THAT. I DID IT BECAUSE IT FELT REALLY...RIGHT. TAKING-A-STEP-TOWARD-WHAT-YOU'VE-ALWAYS-WANTED RIGHT. WE-DON'T-HAVE-TO-EXPLAIN-OURSELVES-BECAUSE-WE-JUST-KNOW RIGHT. OUR-CHILDREN-WILL-NEVER-DOUBT-THEIR-PLACE-IN-THIS-WORLD RIGHT.

AFTER WE HUNG UP, I LAY IN BED AND WHISPERED, *MY HUSBAND, THE NEUROPSYCHOLOGIST.* IT FELT WEIRD. I IMAGINED OUR CHILDREN. IT FELT LESS WEIRD. I WENT TO THE BAR DOWNSTAIRS, WATCHED A BLUEGRASS BAND, AND HOOKED UP WITH THE LEAD SINGER IN AN ALLEY AFTERWARD.
MY PLACE?
SURE.
IT FELT MEDIUM-WEIRD.

OVER THE NEXT FEW DAYS, THE PHONE RANG ALL THE TIME.
IT'S A VERY GOOD IDEA. SHOULD HAVE DONE IT LONG AGO.
I TOLD THEM YOU WOULD GROW UP AND COME TO YOUR SENSES.
WELL, NOW YOU'VE GONE AND DONE IT. EVERYONE HERE IS TOO EXCITED!

I CALLED MY BROTHER.
THIS IS INSANE. ALL OF INDIA HAS CALLED ME IN THE LAST 72 HOURS.
YOU'RE THE ONE WHO SAID YOU WOULD DO IT.
OH WHATEVER, PERFECT SON!
I CAN'T BELIEVE YOU AGREED. IT'S LIKE YOU'VE BEEN TAKEN OVER BY ALIENS.
I HAVEN'T AGREED TO ANYTHING BUT A PHONE CALL.
HOW DOES THIS WORK AGAIN?

HOW IT WORKED

1. MY DAD CALLED THE NEXT MORNING TO GIVE ME THE NEUROPSYCHOLOGIST'S NUMBER.

NO BIGGIE! JUST A CASUAL "HELLO, I AM THE DAUGHTER OF PHILIP JACOB, PERHAPS YOU WOULD LIKE TO MEET ME SOMETIME FOR A CASUAL DINNER IN A PUBLIC SPOT."

DAD.

2. I CALLED.

HI, THIS IS MIRA. MY DAD IS A FRIEND OF YOUR DAD'S. I HEAR YOU ARE UP AT COLUMBIA—I'M DOWN IN WILLIAMSBURG. ANYWAY, LET ME KNOW IF YOU WANT TO GRAB COFFEE OR A DRINK SOMETIME, WOULD LOVE TO MEET UP.

3. I LAY ON THE COUCH, STARED UP AT THE CEILING, AND WAITED FOR MY REAL LIFE TO BEGIN.

9 A.M.
SO?
WHAT?
YOU TALKED?
I LEFT A MESSAGE.
OKAY, GOOD. SO NOW WE WAIT.
THANKS, WASN'T CLEAR ON THAT.
10 A.M.
SO?
MA, YOU GUYS JUST CALLED ME.
I DIDN'T CALL!
DAD CALLED.
WHAT DID YOU TELL HIM?
WHY DON'T YOU JUST ASK HIM?
BECAUSE I'M TALKING TO YOU!

6 P.M.
SO?
I CALLED HIM THIS MORNING. IT'S NOW THE EVENING. HE WILL CALL TOMORROW OR IN A FEW DAYS.
HE DIDN'T CALL YOU BACK SINCE MORNING????
YOU GUYS, THIS IS HOW AMERICAN DATING WORKS. CALM DOWN.

AT THE BAR, THE VIBE WAS OFF.
LET ME GET YOU A DRINK.
I'M ALL GOOD, THANKS.
YOU'RE FROM INDIA, RIGHT?
JUST KIND OF WANT TO SIT HERE AND THINK, THANKS.
THINK IN YOUR OWN APARTMENT.
I WENT BACK UPSTAIRS. NO ONE HAD CALLED. I WENT TO BED.

THAT NIGHT I DREAMED I WAS CHASING A SMALL BROWN BOY ACROSS A LAWN, BUT I WASN'T SURE IF HE WAS MINE OR SOMEONE ELSE'S.

LISTEN, WHO KNOWS ABOUT THIS GUY, OKAY?
WHAT DO YOU MEAN?
I MEAN, COULD BE SOME MADNESS IN THE FAMILY OR SOMETHING. YOU NEVER KNOW.
SHE'S RIGHT. WHO KNOWS WHAT HE WAS REALLY LIKE.
SERIOUSLY? DON'T YOU GUYS WANT TO GIVE HIM A FEW DAYS OR SOMETHING?

Dear Mira,

Well you can't always tell from afar how these boys were raised. You probably escaped a dismal life with that psycho neurologist! His loss.

Sara Kochamma

Dear Sara Kochamma—

I'm fine, don't worry. This is hardly the worst thing that's happened to me. I've been dating in New York for years, remember?

Love,
Mira

IT WASN'T UNTIL A FULL WEEK LATER THAT I FINALLY UNDERSTOOD THE NEUROPSYCHOLOGIST REALLY WASN'T GOING TO CALL. AND THEN I FELT STUPID: STUPID FOR CALLING, STUPID FOR PRETENDING I WAS THE KIND OF PERSON WHO COULD BE HAPPY IN AN ARRANGED MARRIAGE. EXCEPT I HADN'T REALLY BEEN PRETENDING, HAD I? SO STUPID FOR THAT, TOO.
I MEAN, HE PROBABLY IS SOME TOTALLY NORMAL INDIAN GUY WITH AN AMERICAN GIRLFRIEND HE'S BEEN SEEING FOR SEVEN YEARS THAT HIS PARENTS DON'T EVEN KNOW ABOUT.
THAT'S NORMAL?
WHAT.

THAT WINTER WAS LIKE EVERY WINTER IN NEW YORK: TOO COLD, TOO LONG. I BOUGHT MYSELF A MEMBERSHIP TO THE GYM SO I COULD WATCH TELEVISION WHILE I RAN. I WENT ON A FEW STRANGE DATES. MY MOTHER TOOK A TRIP TO INDIA AND CAME BACK WITH THE NEWS.
SO I HEARD ABOUT WHAT HAPPENED WITH THE NEUROPSYCHOLOGIST!
HE FELL INTO A BLACK HOLE AND COULDN'T CALL BACK TO SAY, "SORRY OUR PARENTS PUT YOU UP TO THIS, I'M JUST NOT INTO IT, NO REFLECTION ON YOU"?

IT'S JUST THAT HIS AUNT TALKED TO YOUR AUNT AND SAID, "WE'VE HEARD SHE'S VERY PLAIN, IS IT TRUE?" AND YOUR AUNT SAID, "WELL, SURE, SHE'S NO BEAUTY BUT SHE'S A REALLY NICE GIRL AND—"
WAIT. WHAT?
BECAUSE YOU'RE NOT FAIR, RIGHT? SO THEN THEY DIDN'T WANT YOU. BUT THAT'S ALL.
THAT'S...ALL?
OH, MIR! YOU KNOW HOW IMPORTANT COLOR IS TO SOME SILLY PEOPLE! I MEAN, YOU'RE NEVER GOING TO BE SOMEONE'S TROPHY WIFE, RIGHT? IF THAT'S WHAT THEY WANTED, THEN IT WAS A MISMATCH— THAT'S ALL I'M SAYING.
RIGHT.

I THOUGHT YOU WOULD FEEL BETTER KNOWING IT'S SUCH A DUMB THING! THESE PEOPLE AND THEIR SMALL IDEAS—POOH TO THEM. ANYWAY, YOU LOOK LIKE ME. THAT'S NOT SO BAD, IS IT?
IT'S NOT TRUE.
OF COURSE IT IS! PEOPLE SAY IT ALL THE—
YOU'RE NOT DARK. DAD'S NOT DARK. ARUN'S NOT DARK.
COME ON. YOU THINK YOU ARE SO DIFFERENT FROM US? YOU ARE NOT DIFFERENT FROM US.
WHY WAS THIS THE THING THAT MADE ME WANT TO CRY THE MOST?
I'VE GOTTA GO.

THAT NIGHT, I WANTED TO CALL SOMEONE TO MEET ME, SOMEONE WHO WOULD GET IT, REALLY GET IT. BUT THERE WAS NO ONE TO CALL.
ANYONE SITTING HERE?
NOPE.

THREE YEARS AFTER MOVING TO THE CITY, I RAN INTO A GUY I'D GONE TO SCHOOL WITH BACK IN NEW MEXICO. HE HAD CHANGED A LOT. I HAD CHANGED A LOT. WE EACH MADE SURE THE OTHER PERSON KNEW WE HAD CHANGED A LOT.
I'M A DOCUMENTARY FILM-MAKER. I MAKE MORE EYE CONTACT THAN ANYONE YOU'VE EVER MET.
I'M A WRITER. WHEN I GET NERVOUS I START TO TALK LIKE A WAYWARD NPR HOST.
I DON'T ACTUALLY REMEMBER WHAT WE TALKED ABOUT THAT FIRST NIGHT. INSTEAD I REMEMBER THIS: WALKING OUT OF A BAR IN THE EAST VILLAGE WITH THE MAN FORM OF A BOY I GREW UP WITH. WALKING TO THE SUBWAY. FEELING SURPRISED WHEN HE TOUCHED MY HAND.
I CAN'T BELIEVE YOU REMEMBERED ME.
OF COURSE I REMEMBERED YOU. THERE WERE, LIKE, FIVE INDIANS IN OUR SCHOOL.
SEVEN.

WE SHOULD GO OUT SOMETIME.
WHY? SO YOU CAN SAY YOU TRIED A DARK GIRL? SO YOU CAN TAKE A WALK ON THE WILD SIDE BEFORE GOING BACK TO SOMEONE YOUR MOM WANTS YOU TO MARRY? SO YOU CAN GO THROUGH ME LIKE SOME FUCKING PHASE?
I LIKE TALKING TO YOU.
YEAH, OKAY.

WHEN WE FIRST STARTED DATING, JED DIDN'T WANT ME TO TELL ANYONE WE'D KNOWN EACH OTHER SINCE ELEMENTARY SCHOOL.

IT SOUNDS SO BACKWOODS. YOU MIGHT AS WELL JUST START WHISTLING THE THEME TO *DELIVERANCE*.

YOU'RE JEWISH AND I'M INDIAN! HOW BACKWOODS CAN WE BE?

THE TRUTH WAS WEIRDER. I SPENT TWELVE YEARS OF MY LIFE WITH THE PERSON WHO WOULD BECOME MY HUSBAND AT MY PERIPHERY. IN ELEMENTARY SCHOOL, HE WAS A DARK HEAD RUNNING AROUND THE PLAYGROUND, THE ONE ALL THE KIDS SAID WAS GOING TO HELL BECAUSE THAT'S WHERE JEWS WENT. IN MIDDLE SCHOOL, HE DID A GIRAFFE IMPERSONATION THAT INVOLVED A LOT OF SLOW BLINKING AND LICKING HIS OWN CHIN. IN HIGH SCHOOL, HE SCOWLED FROM COUCHES AT PARTIES AND DEMANDED A SCHOOL-WIDE WALKOUT TO PROTEST THE GULF WAR (ABOUT SIX KIDS FOLLOWED HIM OUT). PEOPLE SAID HE WAS SMART. THEY SAID HE WAS CHEAP. THEY SAID HE WOULD PROBABLY MAKE A LOT MORE MONEY THAN THE REST OF US WHEN HE GREW UP, JUST YOU WAIT.

I DON'T REMEMBER A SINGLE CONVERSATION WE HAD BACK THEN. ALL I KNOW IS THAT WHEN I MET HIM IN NEW YORK, I COULD SEE NEW MEXICO ALL OVER HIM—THE GOOD PARTS, THE PARTS THAT WERE HARD TO EXPLAIN TO ANYONE ELSE, THE PARTS WE WERE TRYING TO ESCAPE. WE STARTED TALKING IN A WAY I'D NEVER BEEN ABLE TO TALK TO ANYONE.
HEY, DO YOU WANT TO—?
YES.

CHAPTER 21: MAN SECRETS, REVEALED!

HOW TO COMMUNICATE WITH MY PARENTS
I TOLD THEM NOT TO CALL BEFORE NOON ON WEEKENDS UNLESS OUR APARTMENT IS ON FIRE.
YOU WHAT?!?!
I SAID, EVEN IF *THEIR* HOUSE IS ON FIRE, THERE'S NOT A TON WE CAN DO, SO THEY MIGHT AS WELL WAIT.
OH MY GOD. YOU'RE INSANE.
NO, I'M THE SON OF A JEWISH MOTHER.
WHAT DOES THAT MEAN?
I'M GOOD AT DISAPPOINTING PEOPLE.

CHAPTER 22: A GIRL LIKE YOU

TOO BAD YOU'RE NOT READY FOR REAL LOVE.
THIS GUY—HE'S NEVER GOING TO REALLY GET YOU. YOU KNOW THAT, RIGHT?
YOU DON'T KNOW EVEN KNOW ME.
I KNOW A GIRL LIKE YOU DOESN'T END UP WITH A WHITE MAN UNLESS SHE WANTS TO BE TREATED LIKE A COLONIZED BITCH.
HEY, SWEETIE!

RIGHT. BECAUSE GOD FORBID MY FALLING IN LOVE ISN'T ABOUT YOUR FEELINGS. GOD FORBID I BECOME HAPPY WITHOUT THE APPROVAL OF SOME MAN WHO THINKS BEING INDIAN GIVES HIM THE RIGHT TO DECIDE WHAT'S BEST FOR ME. GOD FORBID I BECOME SOMEONE ELSE'S COLONIZED BITCH INSTEAD OF YOURS.

FUCK!

HNNH?

NOTHING.

CHAPTER 23: ONLY IN NEW YORK

THE NEXT MORNING, ON MY WAY TO WORK, A BUNCH OF PEOPLE WERE STANDING IN THE MIDDLE OF 7TH AVENUE. I ASKED TWO TEENAGE BOYS WHAT WAS GOING ON.
A PLANE HIT THE WORLD TRADE CENTER.
WHAT? NO WAY.
COMMERCE ST
CHERRY
FUCKING NEW YORK CITY, MAN.

I WENT TO A PAY PHONE AND CALLED MY FATHER.
DAD, YOU'LL NEVER GUESS WHAT JUST HAPPENED OUT HERE.
I AM WATCHING IT ON THE TV! YOU NEED TO GET OUT OF THERE!
DON'T WORRY, IT'S WAY DOWNTOWN. I'M ON 14TH.

NO ONE ON THE STREET SEEMED TOO WORRIED. WE WERE FAR ENOUGH AWAY THAT WE COULD SEE THE GASH IN THE BUILDING, THE SMOKE POURING OUT OF IT, BUT NOT MUCH ELSE.
THEY ARE GOING TO SUE THE PANTS OFF THAT AIRLINE, I'LL TELL YOU THAT.
ONLY IN NEW YORK, KIDS! ONLY IN NEW YORK.
7 AV
MMERCE ST
CHERRY LANE
Phone
<BOOM!>

ARE YOU OKAY?!
DAD, THE...I DON'T...THE OTHER BUILDING JUST CAUGHT FIRE.
IT'S A TERRORIST ATTACK. YOU NEED TO GET OUT OF THERE.
CALM DOWN. THAT'S NOT—
THERE IS ANOTHER PLANE. THEY ARE SHOWING IT ON THE TV. IT JUST HIT THE OTHER BUILDING.
WHAT?
LOOK AT THE FIRE, MIRA. IT WOULD NOT HAVE SPREAD THIS WAY.

THE CELLPHONES WENT DOWN. THE RADIOS WENT DOWN. I STARTED REPEATING WHAT MY DAD WAS SAYING TO A CROWD.
THE FIREMEN ARE THERE BUT THEY CAN'T GET UP THAT HIGH.
PEOPLE ARE JUMPING FROM WINDOWS.
THEY ARE SAYING IT'S A TERRORIST ATTACK.
OH MY GOD.
A WOMAN RAN UP.
PLEASE! MY PHONE ISN'T WORKING! MY HUSBAND IS IN TOWER TWO.

I HANDED HER THE PHONE AND WALKED INTO THE MIDDLE OF 7TH AVENUE WITH EVERYONE ELSE.
THIRTY SECONDS LATER, TOWER TWO FELL.

CHAPTER 24: PAPER CITY

AFTER THE BUILDINGS FELL, THE "MISSING" SIGNS WENT UP.
THEY WENT UP ON SUBWAY WALLS AND IN BODEGAS
AND OVER THE POSTERS
AT MOVIE THEATERS.
OUTSIDE THE HOSPITALS,
THEY BECAME THEIR OWN PAPER CITY.

ON OUR BLOCK, THREE PEOPLE WERE MISSING. ONE I RECOGNIZED BECAUSE HE WAS ALWAYS WALKING HIS DOG AT 2 A.M. WHEN JED AND I WERE COMING HOME. EVERY TIME I SAW HIS POSTER, I WOULD IMAGINE HIM IN THE RUBBLE, WAITING.
ISS
Since Septemb
New York
HANG ON. WE'RE GOING TO FIND YOU.

WE LEARNED NEW NAMES: AL-QAEDA, OSAMA BIN LADEN, KHALID SHEIKH MOHAMMED. ALL DAY, ALL NIGHT, EVERY NIGHT, WE SAW THEIR FACES ON THE TELEVISION.
YOU GUYS ARE RUINING THE FUCKING CITY.
WHAT?
YOU HEARD ME.

THEN ONE NIGHT I SAW A PICTURE OF MYSELF.
MISSING
since before the World Trade Center attack
Last Seen Monday Sept 10th
I BLINKED AND THE WOMAN IN IT BECAME SOMEONE ELSE. SHE HAD A SURIANI NAME LIKE MINE. SHE HAD A LOW FOREHEAD LIKE MINE. SHE WAS A DOCTOR AND LIVED NEAR THE TWIN TOWERS. HER HUSBAND WAS LOOKING FOR HER.
SHE WENT MISSING THE DAY BEFORE THE BUILDINGS FELL.
WHO WAS LEFT TO LOOK FOR ONE MISSING PERSON WHEN 3,000 FOLLOWED HER?

LATER, MY MOM WOULD CALL TO TELL ME SHE WAS A FAMILY FRIEND'S NIECE.
THERE HAS TO BE SOMETHING TO DO!
DOWNTOWN IS STILL BURNING, MOM. THE WIND BLOWS AND HALF OF IT IS PAPERS FROM PEOPLE'S DESKS.
SHE'S A DOCTOR! SHE'S MARRIED! PEOPLE DON'T JUST DISAPPEAR.
DID YOU JUST SAY THAT?
YOU KNOW WHAT I MEAN.
EVERY NIGHT JED AND I WOULD CRAWL INTO BED EARLY AND NOT SLEEP.
HER HUSBAND MUST BE GOING CRAZY.
SWEETIE, THIS ISN'T GOING TO HELP.

AFTER A WEEK, I STOPPED WATCHING TELEVISION. I WENT TO SOUP KITCHENS AND SERVED FIREFIGHTERS A FEW TIMES, AND THEN THERE WERE TOO MANY OF US AND I STOPPED DOING THAT, TOO.

NO ONE WAS COMING OUT OF THE RUBBLE. THE RESCUE CREWS FROM OTHER STATES WERE GOING HOME.

MY DAD CALLED A LOT.

ARE YOU HOLDING UP OKAY?

JESUS, I'M FINE. NOTHING HAPPENED TO ME.

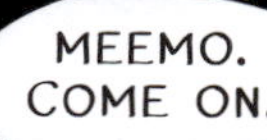

MEEMO. COME ON.

PEOPLE LOST EVERYTHING, DAD.

THAT MONTH, MY NEIGHBORS STARTED SAYING HI TO EACH OTHER MORE. ONCE, WHEN MY GROCERY BAG BROKE ON THE STREET, FOUR DIFFERENT PEOPLE HELPED ME PICK EVERYTHING UP.
IS SHE OKAY?
MY BOYFRIEND IS RUNNING TO GET HER ANOTHER BAG FROM THE CORNER.
YOU GOT THAT, HONEY?
EVERYONE WANTED TO FIX SOMETHING.

NIGHTS WERE DIFFERENT. PEOPLE DRANK AND THEN THEY GOT WEIRD.
LEAVING ALREADY?
HOW DO WE KNOW YOU AREN'T PLOTTING TO KILL EVERYONE IN HERE IF YOU WON'T EVEN TALK TO US?
FINE, GET THE FUCK OUT.
STOP

IN EARLY OCTOBER, I WAS STANDING IN UNION SQUARE WHEN A WOMAN GRABBED MY HAND. SHE DID NOT SPEAK ENGLISH. SHE NEEDED HELP.
COME!
WHAT? WHAT HAPPENED?
COME, COME!
ARE YOU OKAY?

SHE DRAGGED ME TO THE WALL, AND I KNEW BEFORE SHE EVEN POINTED.
YOU.
THAT'S NOT ME.
YOU!
NO, I KNOW. IT'S NOT ME.
NO?
NO.
SHE SHOOK HER HEAD AND SIGHED. WE LOOKED AT THE PICTURE. WE WERE STILL HOLDING HANDS. THE WOMAN IN IT LOOKED BACK AT US AND WE CRIED.

CHAPTER 25: SEPTEMBER 2016

I'M SORRY. I THINK I ALWAYS GET A LITTLE WEIRD AT THIS TIME OF YEAR.
BECAUSE OF 9/11?
YEAH.
BECAUSE IT MADE YOU SCARED OF TERRORISTS?
YEAH, OF TERRORISTS. OF SOME AMERICANS.
WHY?
WHY? WHY.
WHAT?
NOTHING.

I GUESS AMERICA GOT KIND OF WEIRD FOR US FOR A WHILE. PEOPLE DIDN'T LIKE US. ME, APPA, UNCLE ARUN. A LOT OF PEOPLE WHO LOOK LIKE US. MUSLIMS. SIKHS.
WHAT ABOUT AMMA?
NAH. NO ONE EVER THINKS AMMA COULD DO ANYTHING BAD.
BUT SHE'S THE SNEAKY ONE!
TELL ME ABOUT IT.

DID ANYONE EVER TRY TO HURT YOU?
ONCE, A GROUP OF BLACK TEENAGERS SPAT ON ME.
ONCE, A WHITE COUPLE AT A DINER SAID THEY DIDN'T FEEL SAFE NEAR ME AND THE WAITRESS MOVED THEM.
ONCE, A MAN I WAS TRYING TO IGNORE ON THE SUBWAY GRABBED ME BY THE HAIR AND BETWEEN MY LEGS AND YELLED, "SPEAK ENGLISH, YOU DIRTY CUNT!" AND EVERYONE JUST WATCHED AND SAID NOTHING AND I'VE NEVER KNOWN IF IT WAS BECAUSE IT WAS RIGHT AFTER 9/11 OR BECAUSE HE WAS JUST NUTS BUT I WILL REMEMBER ALL THOSE FACES PRETENDING THEY SAW NOTHING FOR THE REST OF MY LIFE.
NOT REALLY.

THE RADIO SAYS DONALD TRUMP IS A BULLY.
YEAH.
BULLIES ARE BAD.
FOR SURE.
DADDY SAYS SOMETIMES IT'S OKAY TO PUNCH A BULLY AS HARD AS YOU CAN.
DOES HE?
BECAUSE THAT'S WHAT BULLIES UNDERSTAND.
NOT SURE HOW I FEEL ABOUT THAT.
DADDY SAID YOU WOULD SAY THAT.

DOES DONALD TRUMP HATE MUSLIMS?
I THINK IT'S MORE LIKE...HE IS ANGRY BECAUSE HE IS SCARED OF TERRORISTS. AND HE THINKS ALL TERRORISTS ARE MUSLIM.
SO THEY SHOULD STOP SCARING HIM!
BUT THEY'RE NOT SCARING HIM. HIS IMAGINATION IS SCARING HIM. MOST OF THEM ARE JUST PEOPLE WITH FAMILIES LIKE US, BUT HE DOESN'T WANT TO BELIEVE THAT.
I HAVE A MUSLIM NAME, RIGHT?
YUP.
SO WILL HE BE ANGRY WITH ME IF HE BECOMES PRESIDENT?

LOOK, YOU ARE AN AMERICAN CITIZEN, OKAY?
WHAT?
YOU ARE EVERY BIT AS AMERICAN AS DONALD TRUMP. THIS COUNTRY IS AS MUCH YOURS AS IT IS HIS AND YOU HAVE EVERY RIGHT TO BE HERE.
ARE YOU SURE?
YES.

HAVE YOU EVER PUNCHED SOMEONE?
COUPLE TIMES. DON'T RECOMMEND IT.
WAS IT BULLIES?
YES.
I'M IN THE CIA, YOU KNOW.
OH YEAH?
AND ALSO THE FBI. AND ALSO I'M THE HEAD OF THE ARMY.
WOW. THAT'S A LOT OF POWER FOR A 7-YEAR-OLD, ISN'T IT?
I'M JUST SAYING, DON'T WORRY. I WILL PROTECT US.

CHAPTER 26: IMPOSTER SYNDROME

SPRING 2002. THE BUILDINGS DOWNTOWN WERE STILL BURNING. I WAS JUST OUT OF GRAD SCHOOL WITH AN MFA, A LOT OF DEBT, AND FOUR FREELANCE JOBS. A FRIEND IN PUBLISHING CALLED WITH AN OFFER.
I CAN'T TAKE IT ON, BUT YOU CAN. IT'S WRITER-FOR-HIRE WORK. SHE HAS SOME BIG NOVEL IDEA BUT NEEDS HELP WITH THE ACTUAL WRITING. SHE USED TO BE A MAGAZINE EDITOR. YOU INTERESTED?
YES. WAIT. WHAT'S THE NOVEL IDEA?
I'LL LET HER TELL YOU.

FREELANCING MEANT WEARING PAJAMAS AND SEEING NO ONE FOR DAYS. I PUT ON LIPSTICK AND PUMPS BEFORE I CALLED BREE.
OH, FANTASTIC! SO YOU'RE A NOVELIST?
MORE OR LESS.*
BECAUSE I HAVE THE ENTIRE STORY ALL WORKED OUT, I BASICALLY JUST NEED SOMEONE WHO CAN FINESSE A BIT.
I CAN FINESSE!
* LESS
WE FOUND OUT WE HAD MANY THINGS IN COMMON. BREE HAD ALSO LIVED IN THE CITY IN HER 20s! WE BOTH LOVED READING! HER COUSIN AND I WENT TO THE SAME COLLEGE!
DO YOU WANT TO MEET NEXT WEEK? I CAN POP DOWN TO OUR APARTMENT IN THE CITY IF YOU COULD MEET ME THERE. IT'S JUST OFF THE PARK.
SURE.

THE NEXT WEEK, ON THE SUBWAY UPTOWN, I MADE A LIST ABOUT HOW I WOULD SPEND THE MONEY IF I GOT THE JOB.
1) student loans
2) groceries
3) health insurance
4) riding taxis like they do in the movies
5) gym membership
6) full-body laser hair removal
7) down payment on Brooklyn brownstone

THE DOORMAN WORE WHITE GLOVES AND CALLED TO ANNOUNCE ME. BREE WORE THE BRIGHTLY COLORED LOAFERS RICH PEOPLE WEAR TO SHOW YOU THEY DON'T TAKE THEIR MONEY TOO SERIOUSLY.
CAN I HELP YOU?
THE DOORMAN SENT ME UP.
I'M MIRA?
OH! OKAY. OF COURSE. RIGHT. YOU DIDN'T SAY...I DIDN'T...BUT THAT'S GREAT! THAT'S WONDERFUL.

INSIDE, THE APARTMENT SMELLED LIKE GARDENIAS.
YOU MUST HAVE COME SUCH A LONG WAY.
WE'RE JUST DOWN IN CHELSEA.
WE?
I LIVE WITH MY BOYFRIEND.
GREAT! AND IS HE ALSO—
A WRITER? NO, HE MAKES DOCUMENTARIES.
NO, I MEANT...
OH! INDIAN? NO.
INDIAN!

WE SAT IN THE LIVING ROOM. IT WAS VERY QUIET.
SO...UM. I CAN'T EVEN THINK OF WHERE TO START.
WELL, SO THE BOOK IS ABOUT MY FAMILY. YOU'RE FAMILIAR WITH THIS COUNTRY'S FOUNDING FATHERS?
SURE.
SO WE'RE ONE OF THE ORIGINAL FOUNDING FAMILIES OF AMERICA.
OH, WOW!
SO THAT'S THE STORY, REALLY.

SO WHAT DID YOUR FAMILY DO?
I JUST TOLD YOU.
YES! NO, I JUST MEAN, SPECIFICALLY. DURING THE REVOLUTION. OR, WELL, DID YOU WANT TO START THERE?
I WANT IT TO START AT THE BEGINNING. I HAVE A LOT OF RESEARCH.
OH, GREAT! RESEARCH!
ACTUALLY, CAN WE BACK UP? I THINK WE'RE GETTING A LITTLE AHEAD OF OURSELVES.
OF COURSE. I'M SORRY.

THIS IS GOING TO BE A BIG BOOK. YOU SHOULD KNOW THAT UP FRONT.
IN FACT, IT WILL PROBABLY HAVE TO BE A TRILOGY. THAT'S HOW I ENVISION IT WORKING BEST.
SO THE RIGHT PERSON IS GOING TO NEED TO BE COMMITTED TO SEEING THE PROJECT ALL THE WAY THROUGH.
IS THAT GOING TO BE A PROBLEM FOR YOU?
I'M WILLING TO JUGGLE THINGS FOR THE RIGHT PROJECT.

I'M ALSO TALKING TO A FRIEND IN TELEVISION ABOUT THE MINISERIES. YOU ALSO WRITE SCREEN-PLAYS, RIGHT?
NO.
OH.
I JUST MEAN, I HAVEN'T YET. BUT I COULD. VERY EASILY.* THAT IS DOABLE.
WELL, I GUESS LET'S JUST CROSS THAT BRIDGE WHEN WE COME TO IT.
OKAY.
* NOPE.

WE DECIDED I WOULD START ON A TRIAL BASIS THE FOLLOWING WEEK. SHE GAVE ME A BOX OF RESEARCH TO TAKE HOME WITH ME.
I WISH I COULD STAY AND GO THROUGH IT WITH YOU, BUT I JUST CAN'T LEAVE THE HOUSE AND KIDS FOR THAT LONG.
OH, COOL. YOU HAVE KIDS?
YES, TH— THREE. BUT MY YOUNGEST DIED A FEW YEARS AGO.
OF CANCER.
SHE WAS TWO.
I'M SO SORRY.

LISTEN, I HAVE TO APOLOGIZE. I WAS A LITTLE THROWN WHEN YOU ARRIVED.
OH, THAT'S NOT...DON'T WORRY ABOUT IT.
THE TRUTH IS, I'M GLAD YOU'RE HALF INDIAN.
I'M WHOLE INDIAN.
I FEEL LIKE WE REALLY CONNECT. I LOVE YOGA, AND I REALLY APPRECIATE THE SPIRITUALITY YOU'LL BE BRINGING TO THIS.
SEE YOU NEXT WEEK?
GREAT!

ON THE WAY HOME, I BOUGHT US ARTICHOKES TO CELEBRATE EVEN THOUGH THEY WEREN'T ON SALE OR FILLING.

A TRILOGY?

JED, SHE SAID IT COULD TAKE YEARS.

WHAT'S IT ABOUT?

HER FAMILY WAS ONE OF THE FOUNDING FAMILIES!

YEAH, BUT WHAT'S THE ACTUAL—

AND SHE WANTS ME TO WRITE THE MINISERIES!

THERE'S A MINISERIES?

AND I ASKED FOR $50 AN HOUR AND SHE SAID YES!!!

COOL.

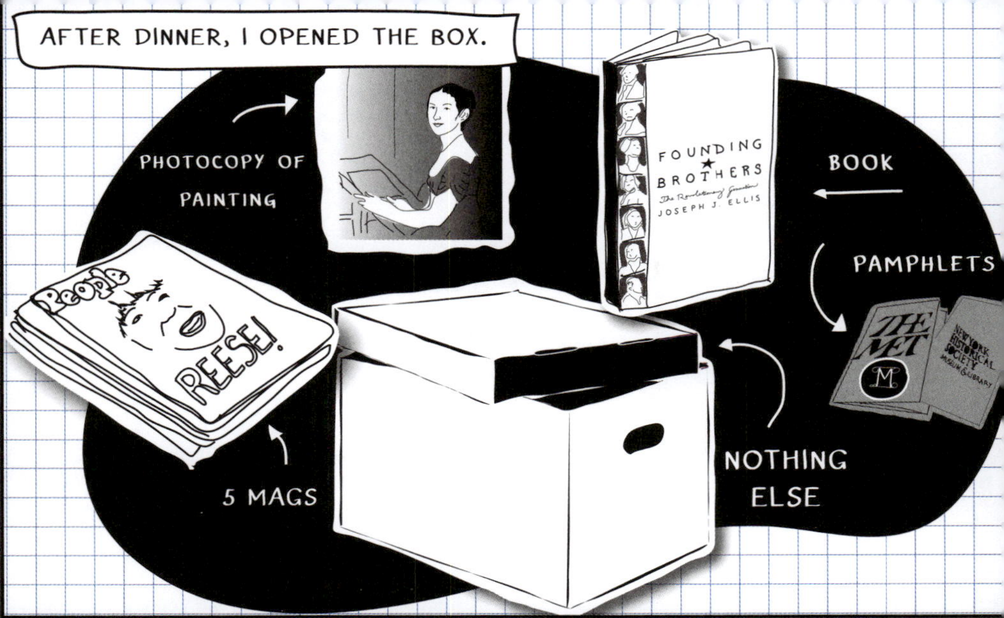

AFTER DINNER, I OPENED THE BOX.

PHOTOCOPY OF PAINTING

FOUNDING ★ BROTHERS
The Revolutionary Generation
JOSEPH J. ELLIS

BOOK

PAMPHLETS

THE MET

M

NEW YORK HISTORICAL SOCIETY
MUSEUM & LIBRARY

People

REESE!

5 MAGS

NOTHING ELSE

OH MY GOD.

RICH PEOPLE.

I MEAN, THERE MUST BE SOMETHING MORE, RIGHT? SHE CAN'T THINK THAT IS, LIKE, THE STORY. RIGHT?

NO ONE EVER TELLS THEM THEIR IDEAS AREN'T EVEN IDEAS.

DO YOU THINK THERE'S EVEN A MINISERIES?

I THINK SHE THINKS THAT BOX IS A TRILOGY.

THE NEXT WEEK, I HEADED UPTOWN. I MEANT TO RETURN THE BOX AND SAY THANK YOU AND GOODBYE, BUT BY THE TIME I GOT TO BREE'S APARTMENT, I HAD AN IDEA.
YOU WANT ME TO FREE-ASSOCIATE?
I JUST THINK YOU MUST HAVE SO MUCH INFORMATION ABOUT THIS BOOK IN YOUR HEAD THAT YOU DON'T EVEN KNOW IS THERE.
I OPENED UP MY LAPTOP. BREE SAT ON THE COUCH. SHE SHUT HER EYES, TOOK A FEW DEEP BREATHS, AND THEN LOOKED AT ME.
MY FAMILY CHANGED THE COURSE OF HISTORY. WE'VE DONE SO MUCH FOR THIS COUNTRY. WE'VE DONE MUCH MORE THAN THE KENNEDYS. IT'S UNBELIEVABLE HOW MUCH PEOPLE LOVE THEM. WE WERE SO SMART WE HAD TO MARRY EACH OTHER BECAUSE NO ONE ELSE UNDERSTOOD US. NOTHING TERRIBLE, JUST COUSINS WITH COUSINS. THIS BOOK IS GOING TO BE AN OPRAH PICK.
IS THAT ENOUGH?
JUST A FEW QUESTIONS.

WHAT YEAR IS IT?

2002.

I MEAN IN THE STORY. WHERE DO YOU WANT TO START?

OH, I DEFER TO YOU ON THAT.

New York, 1764.

WHO DO YOU SEE AS THE MAIN CHARACTER?

A MAN.

He leaves the tavern too late. He is forever leaving the tavern too late. He knows because Kate tells him so in the morning, as the baby fusses in the gray light of the bedroom.

HE'S A DRUNK?

NO. HE'S MAKING PLANS FOR THE REVOLUTION.

GREAT!

THREE HOURS LATER, I HAD WRITTEN A SCENE IN A TAVERN AND ANOTHER AT A FALL FESTIVAL.
THIS IS INCREDIBLE.
YEAH?
WHAT'S...THE STAMP ACT?
WHEN THE BRITISH TAXED—
OH, OF COURSE! THAT WAS IN MY NOTES, RIGHT?
I THINK SO.*
* NOPE.
YOU KNOW, WHEN THINGS REALLY RAMP UP FOR US, YOU SHOULD THINK ABOUT LIVING HERE.
IN YOUR APARTMENT?
JUST TO MAKE THINGS EASIER FOR YOU. IT'S PROBABLY A MUCH EASIER PLACE TO GET THE WORK DONE. YOU KNOW, QUIET.
CHELSEA'S PRETTY... QUIET.
I JUST WANT YOU TO KNOW MY DOOR IS ALWAYS OPEN TO YOU, SHOULD YOU EVER NEED IT.

JESUS CHRIST, WHERE DOES SHE THINK YOU'RE LIVING, IN THE SUBWAY?
I MEAN, SO I HAVE TO MAKE THE WHOLE THING UP. IS THAT SO BAD?
SHE KNOWS WE HAVE JOBS AND, LIKE, PAY RENT, RIGHT? OR DOES SHE NOT KNOW PEOPLE WHO ACTUALLY WORK?
THIS IS JUST WRITING FICTION, RIGHT? IT'S NOT, LIKE, UNETHICAL OR ANYTHING.

THE NEXT WEEK, I CAME IN, SAT DOWN, AND OPENED THE FILE ON THE COMPUTER.
WHAT ARE YOU DOING?
I HAD AN IDEA FOR A SCENE AND I WANTED TO GET IT DOWN REAL FAST.
BUT YOU HAVEN'T ASKED ME ANYTHING YET.
RIGHT. OF COURSE. I'M SORRY.

SOMEONE SHOULD LOSE A CHILD. A LOT OF CHILDREN DIED IN THOSE EARLY YEARS.
THOSE POOR MOTHERS. THAT'S ONE THING ABOUT MY FAMILY LEGACY, WE KNOW LOSS. PEOPLE NEVER GET THAT. THEY JUST SEE MONEY.
DO SOME MORE ABOUT THE REVOLUTION. MORE PLANNING IN THE TAVERN. IS THAT ENOUGH?
THAT'S GREAT, THANKS.

THAT AFTERNOON, I WROTE ABOUT A FARMSTEAD, A FAVORITE SON WITH A FEVER, A MOTHER AND AN OLDER SISTER ARGUING ABOUT WHAT WOULD HELP HIM.

cing outside his door, her soft ste
"Maggie, please."
The steps stop. Outside, a strong
ivers, wraps her shawl tighter. Th
"Child, can you not find some w
out isn't going to make him bette
"Shall I |

OH! DID I TELL YOU ABOUT THE MOTHER AT MY SON'S SCHOOL?

WHAT?

SHE'S HALF INDIAN, TOO! I TOLD HER ALL ABOUT YOU.

naking him look like a ghoul and
with typical anxiousness, has beg
noying her mother.

d blows against the wall, . Elizabe
moans. The shuffling starts agai
occupy yourself? Your scurrying

I KEEP TELLING MY FRIENDS, GET USED TO IT. OUR BOYS WILL PROBABLY MARRY ONE OF THESE ADOPTED CHINESE GIRLS, YOU KNOW? AND WE SHOULD BE PROUD! THEY'RE SO SMART!

HEY, BREE? IT'S KIND OF HARD FOR ME TO WRITE AND TALK AT THE SAME TIME.

OH, SORRY.

A FEW HOURS LATER I HANDED HER THE PRINTED PAGES. AFTER SHE READ THEM, SHE LEFT THEM TURNED OVER IN HER LAP.
WHAT'S WRONG?
IT'S JUST...YOU ARE WRITING EXACTLY WHAT I'VE IMAGINED.
OH, GOOD!
I'M NOT SURE HOW YOU'RE DOING IT. IT'S LIKE YOU'RE JUST TAKING IT FROM ME.

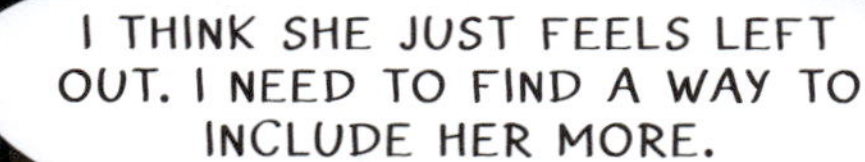
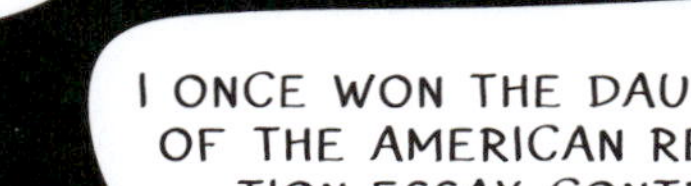

SHE SAID IT LIKE THAT? LIKE YOU WERE STEALING SOMETHING?
I THINK SHE JUST FEELS LEFT OUT. I NEED TO FIND A WAY TO INCLUDE HER MORE.
LIKE WHAT? COMPOSE A SONG CALLED "YOU BRING SOMETHING TO THE TABLE"?
SHE BROUGHT A FOUNDING FAMILY!
MIRA, C'MON. THIS IS NUTS. YOU REALLY WANT TO SPEND YEARS OF YOUR LIFE DOING THIS? ARE YOU EVEN INTERESTED IN THE FOUNDING FAMILIES?
I ONCE WON THE DAUGHTERS OF THE AMERICAN REVOLUTION ESSAY CONTEST!
WHAT ABOUT YOUR OWN WRITING?
YOU MEAN THE STUFF THAT NO ONE WANTS AND DOESN'T PAY?

THE THIRD TIME I WENT UPTOWN, I SAT WITH HER ON THE FLOOR AND TOOK NOTES.
I COULDN'T STOP THINKING ABOUT THE AUTUMN FESTIVAL ALL WEEKEND. I THINK THE COUPLE SHOULD FALL IN LOVE. I WANT YOU TO WRITE THEM FALLING IN LOVE.
YUP.
I MET MY HUSBAND AT YALE. HE DOESN'T THINK THIS BOOK WILL AMOUNT TO ANYTHING. HE DOESN'T SAY THAT, BUT I KNOW. WE HAVEN'T BEEN THE SAME SINCE...THEY SAY IT TAKES TIME.
DOES YOUR HUSBAND BELIEVE IN YOUR WRITING?
WE'RE NOT— YES.
SEE, THAT IS THE DIFFERENCE BETWEEN YOU AND ME. I'VE NEVER HAD THAT KIND OF SUPPORT.

I TRIED TO WRITE THE COUPLE FALLING IN LOVE OVER A HOLIDAY DINNER, BUT IT WAS HORRIBLE. I TRIED TO WRITE THEM FALLING IN LOVE AT A BLACKSMITH'S. IT WAS WORSE. I KEPT THINKING BREE WAS WATCHING ME BUT EVERY TIME I LOOKED OVER SHE WASN'T. I THOUGHT MAYBE I DID NOT KNOW ENOUGH ABOUT BLACKSMITHS. I MADE A LIST OF QUESTIONS I HAD ABOUT BLACKSMITHS. BREE TAPPED ME ON THE SHOULDER. THE LIGHT HAD SHIFTED.
WE NEED TO TALK.
SURE!
THIS IS HARD FOR ME, BUT MY HUSBAND AND I AGREED THAT I JUST NEEDED TO COME RIGHT OUT AND SAY IT.
OKAY.
I'M JUST NOT COMFORTABLE WITH THIS ARRANGEMENT.

I FEEL LIKE YOU'RE TAKING ADVANTAGE OF ME. MY IDEAS. MY WORK. I FEEL LIKE YOU'RE USING THEM WITHOUT REALLY ASKING MY PERMISSION.
YOU HIRED ME TO WRITE THE BOOK.
MY BOOK.
YOUR BOOK.
I MEAN, HOW DO I KNOW YOU'RE NOT JUST GOING TO WALK AWAY WITH EVERYTHING I'VE ALREADY GIVEN YOU? I'M SURE IT HAS OCCURRED TO YOU.

AND LOOK, IT'S NOT THAT I DON'T HAVE SYMPATHY, OKAY? I WOULDN'T BLAME YOU. IT JUST PUTS ME IN A WEIRD POSITION, OBVIOUSLY. I MEAN, IT'S NOT MY NATURE TO BE SUSPICIOUS OF OTHER PEOPLE. I JUST DON'T OPERATE THAT WAY. BUT WHEN YOU SIT HERE FOR HOURS WITHOUT TELLING ME WHAT YOU'RE DOING, OBVIOUSLY I'M GOING TO GET NERVOUS ABOUT IT.
I WAS SCARED TO OPEN MY MOUTH. I WAS SCARED I WOULD START YELLING, AND IF I STARTED YELLING SHE WOULD BE SCARED OF ME, AND IF SHE WAS SCARED OF ME, SHE WOULD BE RIGHT ABOUT ME.

ARE YOU HUNGRY?
WHAT?
YOU MUST BE STARVING! YOU WORKED RIGHT THROUGH LUNCH. WHY DON'T I TAKE US SOME-WHERE NICE?
I INSIST. PLEASE. MY TREAT.
I THINK I SHOULD JUST GO.
WHAT? NO! NO, THAT'S SILLY. WE JUST NEEDED TO TALK ABOUT IT, RIGHT?

I KNEW I SHOULD JUST GET ON THE SUBWAY AND GO HOME AND NEVER COME BACK. I WANTED THE MEAL, THOUGH, AND NOT BECAUSE I WAS HUNGRY. I WANTED BREE TO PAY FOR IT. I WANTED MY EATING IT TO MEAN I WAS GETTING SOMETHING FOR FREE.
WHEN THE FOOD CAME, I ATE TOO MUCH TOO FAST.
I TOLD YOU THAT YOU WERE STARVING! MAYBE ONCE WE'RE DONE WITH THE FIRST CHAPTER, I'LL TAKE US SOMEWHERE TO CELEBRATE. WOULD YOU LIKE THAT?
YOU STILL WANT ME TO DO THE BOOK?
LISTEN, I'M SORRY I SNAPPED AT YOU. I DIDN'T MEAN TO. IT'S JUST THAT IT'S SO IMPORTANT TO ME THAT THIS GOES WELL.

NOTHING HAS GONE WELL IN A LONG TIME. I DON'T EVEN REMEMBER THE LAST TIME IT DID. BUT I KNEW IT WOULD BE LIKE THIS.
AT THE HOSPITAL, I TOLD MYSELF THAT IF GOD WAS GOING TO MAKE ME LIVE WITHOUT HER, IT WAS FOR A REASON. THAT WHATEVER I HAD TO DO ON EARTH WAS BIGGER THAN ME.
THEY GAVE US A CHOICE TO STOP THE TREATMENTS BUT I DIDN'T WANT TO. MY HUSBAND STOPPED COMING.
IN THE END, I HAD TO HOLD HER ARMS AND LEGS DOWN WHILE THEY GAVE HER THE INJECTIONS. SHE WAS SO WEAK SHE COULDN'T EVEN CRY ANYMORE. SHE WOULD JUST STARE AT ME AND TEARS WOULD ROLL DOWN HER FACE.

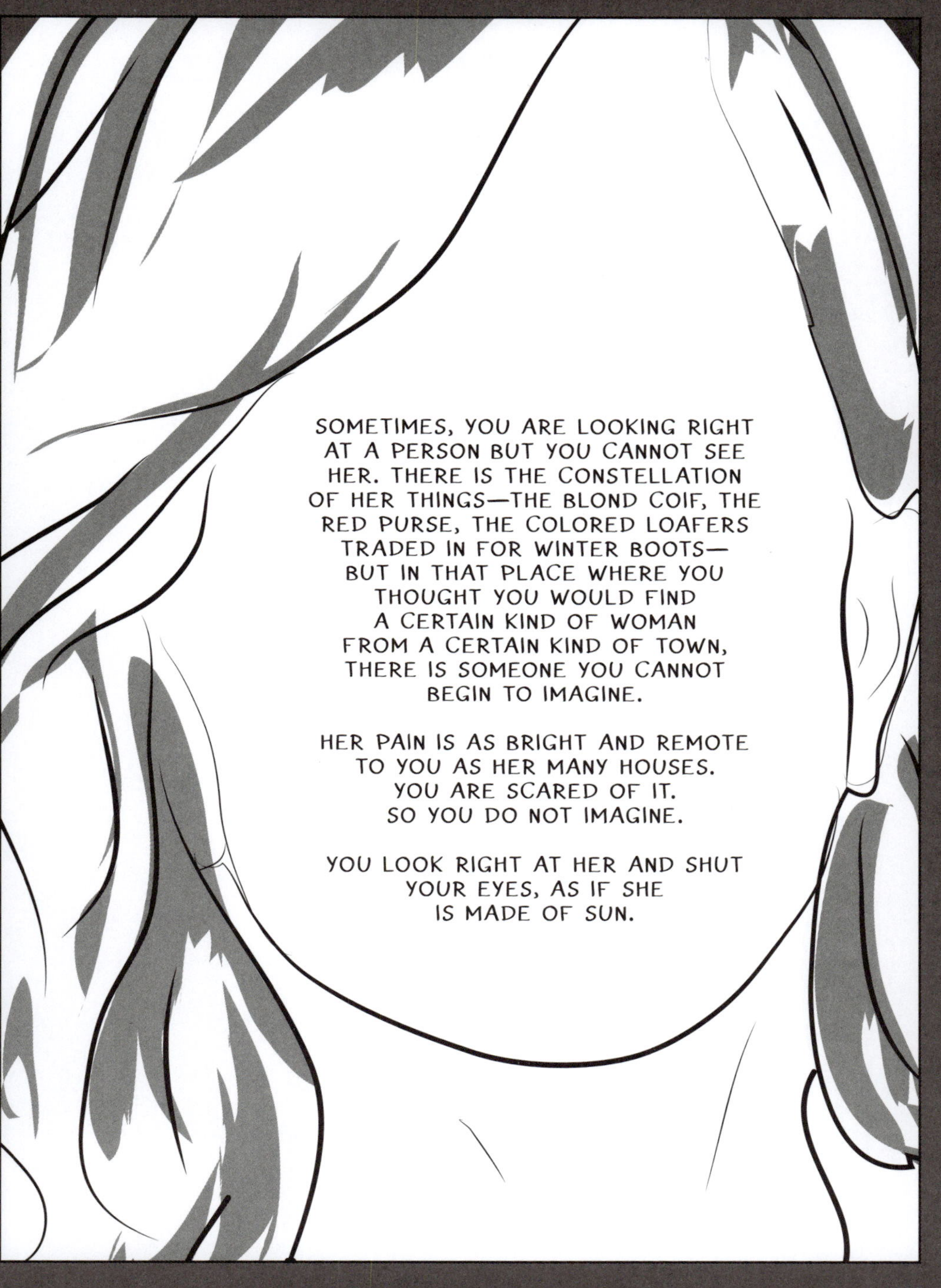
SOMETIMES, YOU ARE LOOKING RIGHT AT A PERSON BUT YOU CANNOT SEE HER. THERE IS THE CONSTELLATION OF HER THINGS—THE BLOND COIF, THE RED PURSE, THE COLORED LOAFERS TRADED IN FOR WINTER BOOTS—BUT IN THAT PLACE WHERE YOU THOUGHT YOU WOULD FIND A CERTAIN KIND OF WOMAN FROM A CERTAIN KIND OF TOWN, THERE IS SOMEONE YOU CANNOT BEGIN TO IMAGINE.
HER PAIN IS AS BRIGHT AND REMOTE TO YOU AS HER MANY HOUSES. YOU ARE SCARED OF IT. SO YOU DO NOT IMAGINE.
YOU LOOK RIGHT AT HER AND SHUT YOUR EYES, AS IF SHE IS MADE OF SUN.

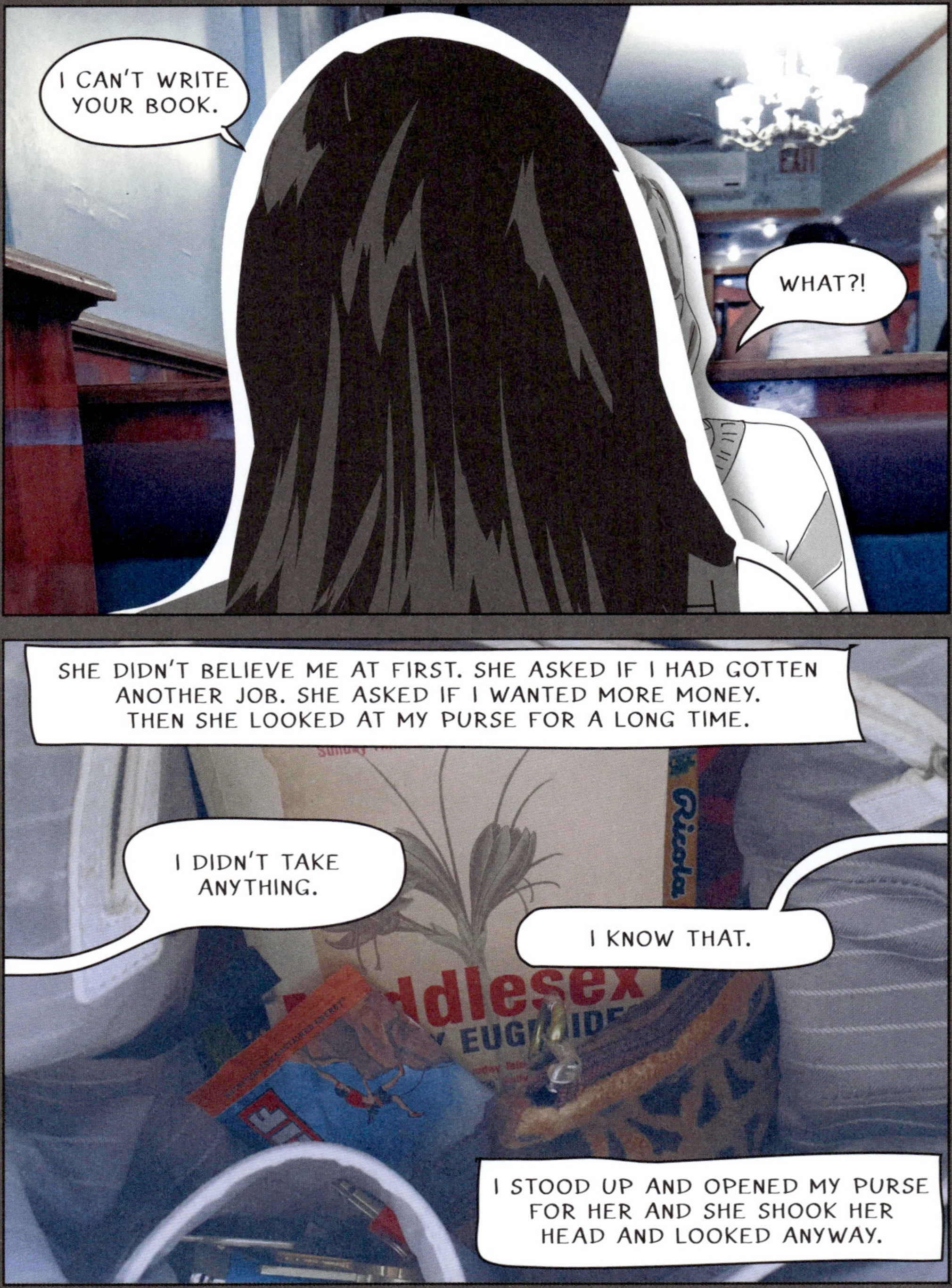

I CAN'T WRITE YOUR BOOK.

WHAT?!

SHE DIDN'T BELIEVE ME AT FIRST. SHE ASKED IF I HAD GOTTEN ANOTHER JOB. SHE ASKED IF I WANTED MORE MONEY. THEN SHE LOOKED AT MY PURSE FOR A LONG TIME.

I DIDN'T TAKE ANYTHING.

I KNOW THAT.

I STOOD UP AND OPENED MY PURSE FOR HER AND SHE SHOOK HER HEAD AND LOOKED ANYWAY.

OUTSIDE THE RESTAURANT, WE STOOD ON THE SIDEWALK, POUNDING OUR FEET TO STAY WARM. IT WAS HARD TO HEAR THROUGH MY HAT.

I WORRY ABOUT YOU, MIRA.

WHAT?

I SAID I HOPE IT ALL WORKS OUT FOR YOU SOMEDAY.

I WILL PRAY FOR YOU.

THANKS.

SHE LOOKED LIKE SHE WAS GOING TO CRY. I SQUEEZED HER ARM AND WALKED TO THE SUBWAY.

YEARS PASSED. I GOT MARRIED. I HAD A BABY. I HAD A FULL-TIME JOB AND A NOVEL I WORKED ON LATE AT NIGHT. BREE BECAME A STORY I TOLD AT PARTIES.

AND SHE KEPT INSISTING I WAS ONLY HALF INDIAN!

NO WAY.

REALLY! NO MATTER HOW MANY TIMES I TOLD HER OTHERWISE.

SO RIDICULOUS.

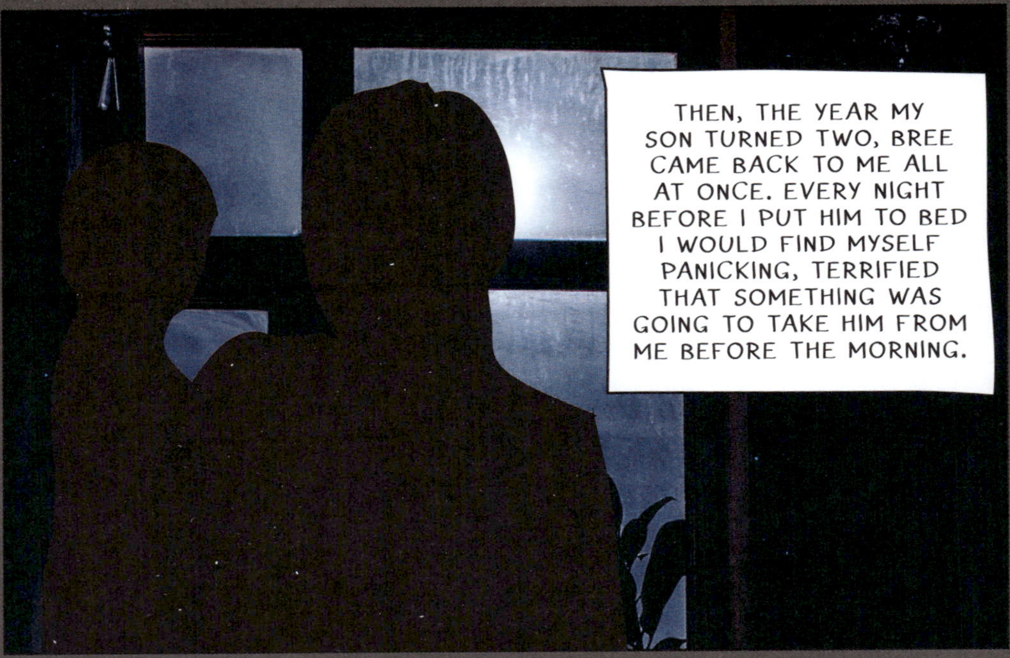

THEN, THE YEAR MY SON TURNED TWO, BREE CAME BACK TO ME ALL AT ONCE. EVERY NIGHT BEFORE I PUT HIM TO BED I WOULD FIND MYSELF PANICKING, TERRIFIED THAT SOMETHING WAS GOING TO TAKE HIM FROM ME BEFORE THE MORNING.

THAT'S WHEN I WOULD SEE HER. HOW HER EYES DARTED FROM SIDE TO SIDE IN EVERY ROOM, ALWAYS SEARCHING FOR SOMETHING. HOW SHE ALWAYS LOOKED RELIEVED WHEN THEY LANDED ON ME. HOW HER FACE HOLLOWED WHEN WE SAID GOODBYE. I WOULD FIND MYSELF WHISPERING TO HER UNDER MY BREATH—A SPELL TO WARD AWAY THE FATE I MIGHT DESERVE.

I DID NOT SEE YOU, EITHER.

I DID NOT EVEN TRY.

CHAPTER 27: MARRIAGE

IN 2002, WE PROTESTED. WE PROTESTED THE VIOLENCE IN NEW YORK AGAINST MUSLIMS AND SIKHS, AND THE AMERICAN GOVERNMENT SENDING BROWN MEN TO GUANTANAMO WITHOUT TRIAL, AND CONGRESS VOTING IN SUPPORT OF A WAR WITH IRAQ EVEN THOUGH IRAQ HAD NOTHING TO DO WITH 9/11. MOSTLY, THOUGH, WE STARED AT EACH OTHER AND WONDERED HOW IT WOULD EVER STOP.

STOP THE WAR ON IRAQ
WE SHOULD GET MARRIED.
WHAT?
I'M SERIOUS.
YOU SURE YOU WANT TO TAKE ON THE LIABILITY?
HA.

I WASN'T JOKING THOUGH.

WHAT?

ABOUT GETTING MARRIED. AMERICA'S NOT SO UP ON MY PEOPLE ANYMORE, IN CASE YOU DIDN'T NOTICE.

OF COURSE I NOTICED. WHAT DOES THAT HAVE TO DO WITH US?

I'M JUST SAYING, IT'S NOT LIKE, ROMANTIC. YOU MARRY ME, YOU MARRY HOW AMERICA TREATS PEOPLE LIKE ME.
YOU THINK I DON'T KNOW THAT?
AND IN WHAT WORLD WOULD I NOT HAVE TO DEAL WITH IT? JEWS AREN'T EXACTY WINNING WORLDWIDE POPULARITY CONTESTS.
BUT IT'S DIFFERENT. YOU CAN BLEND IN IF YOU WANT TO.
RED ZONE
YWCA
BECAUSE I'M WHITE?
YES.

OKAY, BUT WHAT DOES THAT MEAN? WE MARRY PEOPLE WE DON'T LOVE JUST BECAUSE WE'RE MORE LIKE THEM THAN EACH OTHER? FUCK THAT. I DON'T WANT TO BE WITH SOMEONE ELSE.
DO YOU WANT TO BE WITH SOMEONE—?
NOPE.
DO YOU WANT TO BE WITH ME?
OF COURSE I DO.
WELL THEN.

AND YOU NEVER KNOW—THINGS MIGHT REALLY TURN AROUND WITH THE NEXT PRESIDENT.
OH MY GOD, JED.
I'M SERIOUS! REMEMBER HOW BAD IT WAS UNDER BUSH SENIOR? AND THEN CLINTON CAME ALONG AND, YES, HE WAS FLAWED BUT—
—AND NOW IT'S BUSH TWO! AND SHOCK AND AWE! AND EVERYTHING IS WORSE!
YEAH, BUT WHO'S TO SAY THERE ISN'T SOMEONE OUT THERE RIGHT NOW WITH A VISION FOR THIS COUNTRY WE HAVEN'T EVEN IMAGINED? WHO'S TO SAY THAT PERSON WON'T CHANGE THINGS IN WAYS WE NEVER SAW COMING?

MY GOD, WHAT IS IT WITH YOU AND THE OPTIMISM? IS IT, LIKE, GENETIC?
OH, DEFINITELY! I MEAN, WHO IS MORE OPTIMISTIC THAN THE JEWS?
HA.
MAN, THAT 20TH CENTURY WAS LIKE ONE LONG DAY AT THE SPA FOR US!
OKAY, OKAY. I GET IT.
A HEAD MASSAGE! FROM GOD!
SETTLE DOWN, ROTHSTEIN.

CHAPTER 28: OUR FAMILIES GET THE NEWS

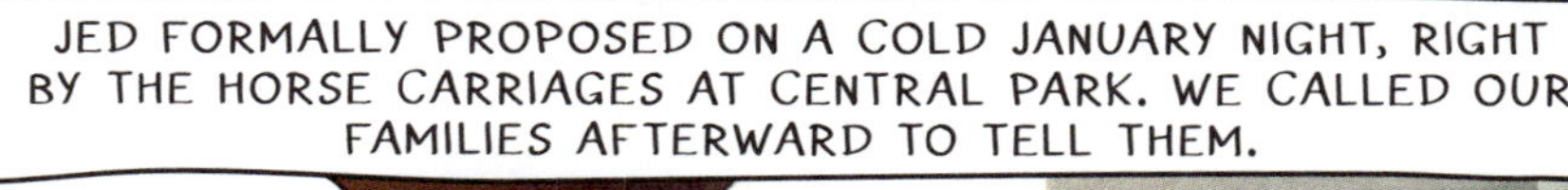

JED FORMALLY PROPOSED ON A COLD JANUARY NIGHT, RIGHT BY THE HORSE CARRIAGES AT CENTRAL PARK. WE CALLED OUR FAMILIES AFTERWARD TO TELL THEM.

THIS IS WONDERFUL! WE LIKE HIM SO MUCH! YOU TWO ARE VERY GOOD TOGETHER.
WONDERFUL! GOODBYE!*
*NOT GREAT WITH EMOTIONS

JED'S PARENTS

WE TOLD OUR FRIENDS. THEY SAID, "OH MY GOD, MIRA JACOB! A NICE JEWISH GIRL! MAZEL TOV!"

WE SAID, "SHE IS NOT JEWISH. IN FACT, SHE IS ABOUT AS NOT JEWISH AS YOU CAN IMAGINE."

BUT WE LOVE YOU VERY MUCH.

BUT ONE GOOD THING ABOUT YOU MARRYING THAT JEW.

AT LEAST THE CHILDREN WILL BE FAIR. SO THAT IS NICE, EVEN IF THEY ARE GOING TO HELL.

CHAPTER 29: SUMMER ON THE TELEVISION

SOMETIMES, WHEN I WAS FEELING BAD ABOUT HAVING PARENTS WHO WOULD NEVER REALLY UNDERSTAND ME, I WOULD LIE IN BED IMAGINING ALL THE EPIPHANIES THE STONED AMERICAN FAMILIES AROUND US WERE HAVING.

DAD, I REALLY JUST DON'T WANT TO BE A DOCTOR.
YOU KNOW, I THINK I ONLY WANTED THAT FOR YOU BECAUSE MY OWN CHILD-HOOD WAS FILLED WITH SO MUCH INSTABILITY, BUT I GET IT. BE A MUSICIAN!
WANT SOME ICE CREAM?

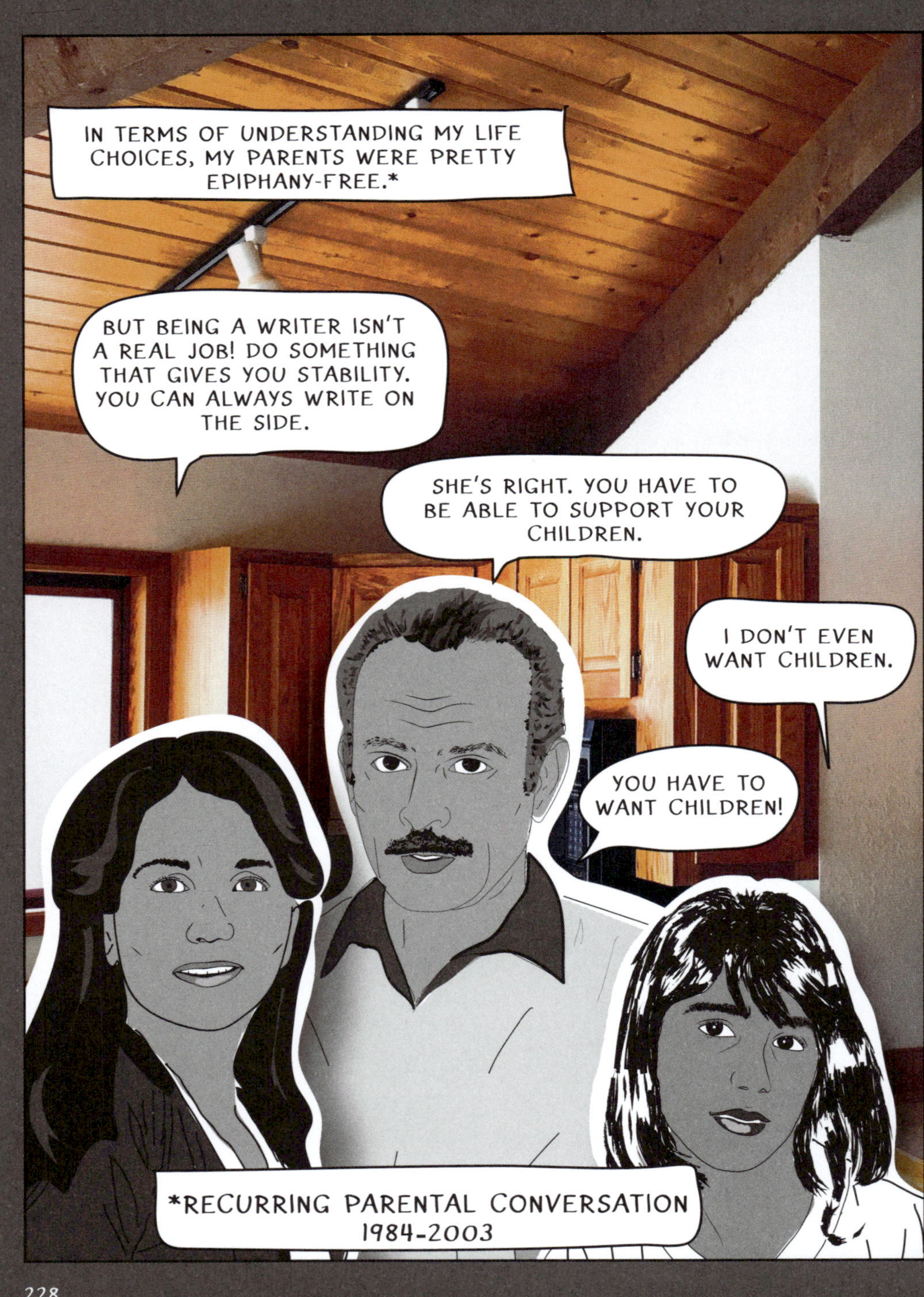
IN TERMS OF UNDERSTANDING MY LIFE CHOICES, MY PARENTS WERE PRETTY EPIPHANY-FREE.*
BUT BEING A WRITER ISN'T A REAL JOB! DO SOMETHING THAT GIVES YOU STABILITY. YOU CAN ALWAYS WRITE ON THE SIDE.
SHE'S RIGHT. YOU HAVE TO BE ABLE TO SUPPORT YOUR CHILDREN.
I DON'T EVEN WANT CHILDREN.
YOU HAVE TO WANT CHILDREN!
*RECURRING PARENTAL CONVERSATION 1984-2003

THE YEAR AFTER I GOT MARRIED, THE RECURRING PARENTAL CONVERSATION STOPPED.
MIRA, I HAVE THE CANCER.
NO.
YES. IT'S GOING TO BE OKAY.
DAD.

MY DAD GETTING CANCER WAS NOT OKAY. IT WAS NOT OKAY THE FIRST YEAR WITH THE FIRST SURGERY, AND BY THE THIRD YEAR, SECOND SURGERY, AND THE FIFTH ROUND OF CHEMO, IT WAS REALLY NOT OKAY.

EAT ONE CHAPATI! JUST ONE!

YOU'RE WASTING AWAY!

I CAN'T.

DAD, HAVE YOU TRIED SMOKING WEED?

ARE YOU NUTS? THE DRUGS WILL KILL HIM!

THINGS YOU DIDN'T IMAGINE DOING IN YOUR 30s

HOUSE OF THE GUY EVERYONE BOUGHT WEED FROM IN HIGH SCHOOL

OH, HEY. DOES, UM, DAVE STILL LIVE HERE?

MY NAME IS COOPER! I AM 6!

THAT'S FANTASTIC! GOODBYE FOREVER, COOPER!

THING YOU DID NOT IMAGINE DOING EVER

UM, HEY, IT'S MIRA. I WAS WONDERING IF YOU KNEW WHERE I COULD GET SOME, UH...

IT'S FOR MY DAD.

GUY WHO WAS ALWAYS HIGH IN HIGH SCHOOL

DUDE. SERIOUSLY?

THAT ONE GUY YOU WENT ON A DATE WITH

WAIT, WHO IS THIS?

ONE OF THE CARPOOL MOMS

YOU BETCHA. COME ON OVER, HONEY.

THE FIRST TIME I BROUGHT WEED HOME, IT DID NOT GO WELL.

OH MY GOD! YOU KNOW THE DRUG DEALERS? WHO SAW YOU DO THIS? THE FBI WILL COME! YOU WILL GET US ARRESTED! DO YOU WANT TO GET US ARRESTED? WHAT KIND OF CHILD ARE YOU??? YOUR MOTHER CANNOT GO TO JAIL FOR A CRIME SHE DID NOT COMMIT! I WILL NOT LET THAT HAPPEN!

MRS. REED GAVE IT TO ME FOR YOU.
MRS. REED DOESN'T—
YES SHE DOES.
NO!
IT'S GOING TO BE OKAY.
MIRA.
GETTING MY DAD HIGH WASN'T EASY AT FIRST.
ABSOLUTELY NOT.
IT WILL HELP YOU EAT.
NO.
IF YOU EAT, MOM WILL BE HAPPY.
GIVE IT TO ME.

THIS IS YOUR DAD ON DRUGS, DAY ONE

CAN I HAVE A LITTLE MORE RICE?

YES! WHAT ELSE?

DO WE HAVE ICE CREAM?

NOBODY MOVE! I AM GOING TO BUY ICE CREAM!

THIS IS YOUR DAD ON DRUGS, WEEK TWO

DO YOU KNOW WHAT IS SO FUNNY? MY OLD FRIEND CHARLES COMES AND SEES ME EVERY DAY AT 4:20 AND DO YOU KNOW WHAT HE WANTS TO DO?

I CAN GUESS.

THIS IS YOUR DAD ON DRUGS, MONTH THREE
CAN YOU BELIEVE THIS GOOGLE EARTH? IT'S A MIRACLE! I CAN SIT HERE IN MY CHAIR AND FLY—PISHOOM!—ANYWHERE IN THE WHOLE ENTIRE WORLD! I WENT TO THE GRAND CANYON AND THEN TO THE FORBIDDEN CITY ALL IN ONE NIGHT! WHAT A TIME TO BE ALIVE! WHAT A BEAUTIFUL LIFE!
DAD.
WHAT?
NOTHING.

ONE NIGHT, MY DAD FINALLY ASKED.
DO YOU WANT SOME?
WHAT? REALLY?
I ALMOST DIDN'T DO IT BECAUSE IT WASN'T REALLY IN CHARACTER WITH WHAT I KNEW OF HIM, BUT THEN NEITHER WAS DYING OF CANCER.

WE GOT HIGH. WE ATE CHIPS AND ICE CREAM AND PEANUT BRITTLE. WE WATCHED TV. WE LAUGHED LOUDLY AND FOR TOO LONG AT EVERYTHING. A COMMERCIAL CAME ON WITH AN OLD MAN DRIVING A LITTLE BOY IN A DARK RED SPORTS CAR. IT WAS SUMMER ON THE TELEVISION. IT WAS WINTER OUTSIDE. SOMETHING POPPED INTO MY MIND, NOT QUITE CLEAR BUT ON THE PERIPHERY, SOMETHING I WOULD UNDERSTAND IF I TURNED AND LOOKED AT IT DIRECTLY. I TURNED AND LOOKED AT MY DAD. HE SAID IT.

I WILL NEVER KNOW YOUR CHILDREN.

IT WAS OUR

EPIPHANY

TWO YEARS AFTER MY DAD DIED, I HAD A SON. THREE YEARS AFTER THAT, I FINISHED MY FIRST NOVEL.
DID APPA LIKE YOUR BOOK?
HE DIED BEFORE I FINISHED IT, SO HE DIDN'T GET TO READ IT.
CAN YOU CARRY ME?

HEY, I HAVE AN IDEA! HOW ABOUT WE GET ALL THE PAGES AND PUT THEM ON THE STOOP AND WHEN A BIG WIND COMES IT WILL BLOW THEM UP INTO HEAVEN, AND THEN APPA CAN READ YOUR BOOK AND IT WILL BE BEAUTIFUL! WHAT DO YOU THINK?
DAD.
WHAT?
NOTHING. GREAT IDEA.

CHAPTER 30: MID-SEPTEMBER 2016

WAIT, WHAT HAPPENED? I DON'T UNDERSTAND.

I SENT MY PARENTS THAT VIDEO FROM THE *TIMES*. ALL THE PEOPLE GETTING BEATEN UP AND ESCORTED OUT OF THE RALLIES. I MEAN, LOOK, THEY CAN'T SUPPORT THIS GUY AND NOT LOOK AT WHAT HE'S DOING TO PEOPLE.

AND THEN?

I...DON'T KNOW. MY MOM TOLD ME MY DAD WAS REALLY UPSET, SO I CALLED. HE SAID TO NEVER SEND THEM ANYTHING LIKE THAT AGAIN.

REALLY?

I DON'T THINK I'VE EVER HEARD HIM THAT ANGRY WITH ME.

BUT IT'S NOT LIKE YOU MADE UP THAT VIDEO.
HE THINKS I DON'T RESPECT THEM, THAT I THINK THEY'RE OLD AND OUT OF TOUCH. BUT I DON'T. I MEAN, I REALLY DON'T. I JUST...
I DON'T UNDERSTAND HOW THEY CAN SEE WHAT THIS GUY IS ABOUT AND SUPPORT HIM! HE'S STOKING RELIGIOUS HATRED! RACIAL HATRED! HOW DO THEY THINK THIS IS GOING TO AFFECT OUR LIVES? THEIR LIVES! ARE THEY FUCKING KIDDING ME?
SHHH.

SO WHERE DID YOU LEAVE IT?
THEY SAID THEY DIDN'T WANT TO DISCUSS IT ANY MORE, PERIOD.
SO WE'RE JUST SUPPOSED TO PRETEND THEM SUPPORTING A RACIST IS NORMAL?
THEY DON'T THINK HE'S RACIST.
OH, WELL THEN.

I DON'T KNOW WHAT TO TELL YOU. I'M SORRY. I FEEL SICK.

BUT THEY WATCHED THE VIDEO? THEY SAW WHAT WAS HAPPENING?
THEY SAID IT'S JUST THE MEDIA MAKING THINGS UP.
WHAT DOES THAT MEAN?
I DON'T KNOW.

CHAPTER 31: THE BARK MITZVAH

RIGHT FROM THE START, I LOVED JED'S FAMILY. MY IN-LAWS WERE WARM AND WELCOMING AND MOSTLY ON THE RIGHT SIDE OF NUTTY.
WE'RE HAVING A "WELCOME TO THE JUNGLE" DINNER! WE'LL HAVE VINES EVERYWHERE AND BANANAS FOSTER FOR DESSERT! DAD SAYS HE ISN'T GOING TO WEAR THE LOINCLOTH I GOT HIM, BUT WE'LL SEE ABOUT THAT.
NO WE WON'T.
SOMETIMES, THOUGH, THINGS COULD GET COMPLICATED...

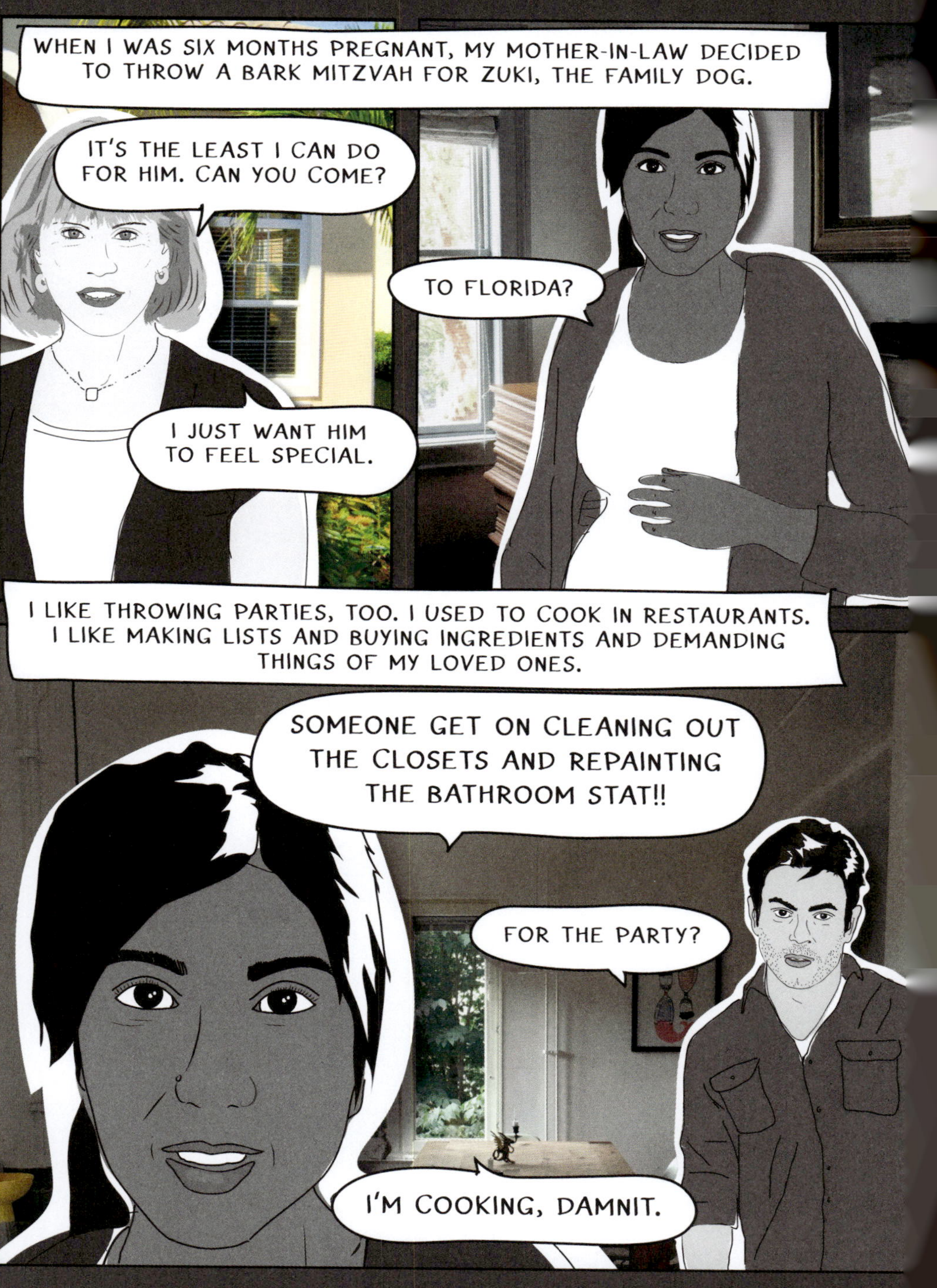
WHEN I WAS SIX MONTHS PREGNANT, MY MOTHER-IN-LAW DECIDED TO THROW A BARK MITZVAH FOR ZUKI, THE FAMILY DOG.
IT'S THE LEAST I CAN DO FOR HIM. CAN YOU COME?
TO FLORIDA?
I JUST WANT HIM TO FEEL SPECIAL.
I LIKE THROWING PARTIES, TOO. I USED TO COOK IN RESTAURANTS. I LIKE MAKING LISTS AND BUYING INGREDIENTS AND DEMANDING THINGS OF MY LOVED ONES.
SOMEONE GET ON CLEANING OUT THE CLOSETS AND REPAINTING THE BATHROOM STAT!!
FOR THE PARTY?
I'M COOKING, DAMNIT.

THE MORNING OF THE BARK MITZVAH WAS BUSY. MY MOTHER-IN-LAW DIDN'T LIKE HER OUTFIT AND ZUKI HAD GOTTEN INTO THE GUEST KIBBLE.
MOM, WHERE DO YOU WANT THE CHEW TOYS?
PLEASE DO NOT PICK UP ANYTHING ELSE!* YOU'RE GIVING ME TSURIS.
*BONE-SHAPED CAKE
*BONE-SHAPED COOKIES
*CHAMPAGNE
*PAW-PRINT PLATES
*NAPKINS WITH "ZUCCHERO R., JUNE 14, 2008" PRINTED ON THEM
*YARMULKES
*DOGGIE YARMULKES
*KIBBLE
*WATER BOWLS

SHE WAS STILL GETTING READY WHEN THE FIRST GUESTS ARRIVED.

HI! WELCOME TO THE BARK MITVAH!

I'M BOB.

DAN.

HAS ANYONE SEEN MY SCOTTIE-PRINT PANTS?

LYNDA WILL BE OUT IN A SEC. CAN I GET YOU SOMETHING TO DRINK? WE'VE GOT COFFEE, CHAMPAGNE, WINE—

WINE.

WINE.

GREAT. BE RIGHT BACK.

A LOT OF SMALL DOGS AND THEIR OWNERS CAME TO THE BARK MITZVAH. SOME OF THEM WERE HAPPIER ABOUT IT THAN OTHERS.

BUTTONS WAYNE SPENT THE FIRST 20 MINUTES GROWLING AT EVERYONE FROM HER OWNER'S LAP. SOMEONE—NO ONE KNEW WHO—PEED IN THE LAUNDRY ROOM. SOMEONE ELSE JUMPED INTO THE POOL.
OSKAR SCHINDLER, YOU KNOW BETTER THAN THAT!

MY MOTHER-IN-LAW'S BEST FRIEND, PAULA, CAME.

HIS TALLIS IS JUST ADORABLE!

NANCY ABRAMS CROCHETED IT!

NANCY'S A DOLL.

I WAS ON MY WAY TO THE KITCHEN WHEN DAN HANDED ME HIS GLASS.
I'LL HAVE A LITTLE MORE WHITE, PLEASE.
OH, SURE! THERE'S AN OPEN BOTTLE ON THE COUNTER.
JUST HALF A GLASS.
HE WENT BACK TO HIS CONVERSATION.
I TOOK THE GLASS. I GOT THE WINE. WHEN I CAME BACK, BOB HELD HIS OUT.
I'LL HAVE ANOTHER, TOO.
I TOOK BOB'S GLASS. I WATCHED MYSELF DO IT AND HATED MYSELF FOR DOING IT AND COULD NOT STOP MYSELF FROM DOING IT.

SOMETIMES, EVERYTHING YOU HAVE EVER LEARNED CAN TURN YOU INTO SOMEONE YOU DON'T WANT TO BE.
JUST A SPLASH, PLEASE.
RIGHT AWAY, SAHIB.

IN THE KITCHEN, I THOUGHT ABOUT BREAKING OFF THE BOTTOM OF THE WINE BOTTLE AND STABBING BOB THROUGH THE NECK WITH IT, BUT THAT SEEMED EXTREME. WHEN I CAME BACK, DAN HELD OUT HIS DIRTY PLATE.
YOU CAN JUST TAKE THAT TO THE KITCHEN.
IF YOU'RE HEADING THAT DIRECTION—
I'M NOT.

I WENT AND STOOD OUTSIDE LOOKING IN AT THE PARTY. I PRESSED MY BELLY AND A FOOT KICKED BACK AND I WONDERED WHAT COLOR IT WAS. A FEW MINUTES LATER, PAULA CAME OUT, TOO.
ARE YOU OKAY, HON? DO YOU NEED TO LIE DOWN?
THEY THINK I'M THE HELP.
WHAT? WHO?
BOB AND DAN. BECAUSE IF I LOOK LIKE ME AND I AM HERE, IT MUST BE TO SERVE THEM.
WAIT, REALLY? ARE YOU SURE?
I LIKE PAULA. SHE IS KIND AND SARCASTIC AND WEARS LARGE NECKLACES AND SAYS THE THING NO ONE ELSE WILL.
WATCH.

I HELD MY BREATH. I WALKED BY DAN AND BOB AS SLOWLY AS POSSIBLE. NOTHING HAPPENED. I IMAGINED PAULA TELLING SOMEONE AT TENNIS THE NEXT DAY ABOUT ME OVERREACTING AND THEN THAT SOMEONE TELLING SOMEONE ELSE, UNTIL THEY COULD ALL JUST SAY WHAT THEY PROBABLY THOUGHT ANYWAY.
HE SHOULD HAVE MARRIED A NICE JEWISH GIRL!!!

THEN, JUST AS I WAS ALMOST OUT OF THE ROOM...

MISS! WAIT, HERE YOU GO.

I REACHED FOR THE DIRTY DISHES LIKE THEY WERE A TROPHY AND TURNED AROUND, SMILING AT PAULA. PAULA COVERED HER FACE WITH HER HANDS. I STOPPED SMILING.

WINNER

AFTER THE CEREMONY HAD BEEN PERFORMED, THE DOGS WERE GIVEN CHOPPED-LIVER MUFFINS IN THE KITCHEN AND MY MOTHER-IN-LAW MADE A TOAST.
...AND AS LONG AS WE ARE CELEBRATING, I WILL JUST SAY THAT I AM SO THRILLED MY DAUGHTER-IN-LAW COULD BE HERE TOO, AND WE CANNOT WAIT TO WELCOME THE NEWEST MEMBER OF OUR FAMILY, EVEN IF THE BABY IS MADE ENTIRELY OF WENDY'S CHICKEN SANDWICHES BECAUSE THAT IS ALL MAMA EVER EATS ANYMORE.
DAN AND BOB LOOKED FROM ONE SIDE OF THE ROOM TO THE OTHER AND BACK UNTIL MY MOTHER-IN-LAW HUGGED ME. THEN THEY LOOKED AT ME.

BY THE END OF THE PARTY, I WAS EXHAUSTED.

THANKS FOR COMING, DAN.

I HAD NO IDEA YOU HAD SUCH AN EXOTIC DAUGHTER-IN-LAW! WHAT A BEAUTIFUL GIRL SHE IS!

HE SAID IT TO HER BUT LOOKED AT ME. I STARED AT HIM UNTIL HE WALKED AWAY.

YOU KNOW HE WAS JUST GIVING YOU A COMPLIMENT, RIGHT?

RIGHT.

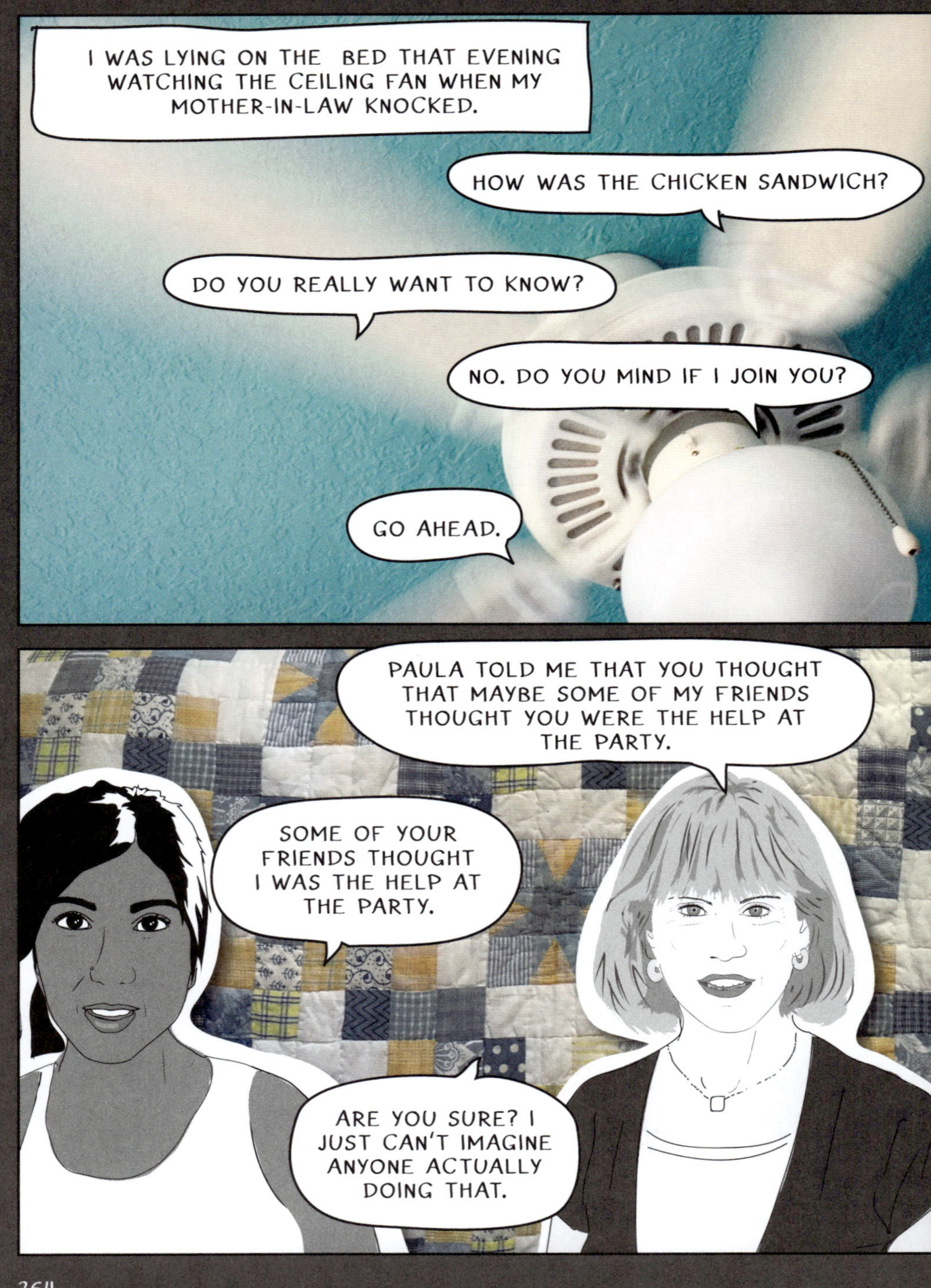
I WAS LYING ON THE BED THAT EVENING WATCHING THE CEILING FAN WHEN MY MOTHER-IN-LAW KNOCKED.
HOW WAS THE CHICKEN SANDWICH?
DO YOU REALLY WANT TO KNOW?
NO. DO YOU MIND IF I JOIN YOU?
GO AHEAD.
PAULA TOLD ME THAT YOU THOUGHT THAT MAYBE SOME OF MY FRIENDS THOUGHT YOU WERE THE HELP AT THE PARTY.
SOME OF YOUR FRIENDS THOUGHT I WAS THE HELP AT THE PARTY.
ARE YOU SURE? I JUST CAN'T IMAGINE ANYONE ACTUALLY DOING THAT.

SOMETIMES, YOU GO ALONG WITH IT AND PRETEND NOTHING HAPPENED. SOMETIMES, YOU HOLD YOUR BREATH UNTIL THE FEELING OF WANTING TO BE BELIEVED PASSES. SOMETIMES, YOU WEIGH EXPLAINING AGAINST STAYING QUIET AND KNOW THEY'RE BOTH JUST DIFFERENT KINDS OF HEAVY. SOMETIMES, WHEN IT'S YOUR MOTHER-IN-LAW—A WOMAN YOU STARTED CALLING MOM THE DAY YOU GOT ENGAGED BECAUSE YOU ADMIRED THE FEROCITY WITH WHICH SHE LOVED HER CHILDREN, AND MAYBE EVEN WANTED SOME OF IT FOR YOURSELF—YOU LOOK AHEAD AND SEE ALL THE YEARS OF BIRTHDAYS AND GRADUATIONS AND WEDDINGS THAT WILL BE SHADOWED BY THINGS THAT SHE CAN'T IMAGINE ABOUT YOUR LIFE. SOMETIMES, YOU CAN'T HOLD YOUR BREATH LONG ENOUGH.

NO.
WE CAN TALK, BUT NOT ABOUT HOW I DON'T KNOW WHAT HAPPENED.
YOU WERE LOOKING FOR YOUR SCOTTIE-PRINT PANTS.

WHAT?
OH GOD. I'M SORRY.
WHAT KINDS OF JERKS EXPECT A PREGNANT WOMAN TO WAIT ON THEM?
I FEEL AWFUL.
I WISH I HAD KNOWN! I SHOULD HAVE INTRODUCED YOU AS MY DAUGHTER RIGHT AWAY! I WOULD HAVE SAID, "THIS IS MY DAUGHTER, MIRA." I DON'T KNOW WHY I DIDN'T SAY THAT!

I JUST THOUGHT EVERYONE KNEW. UGH, WHY DID I EVEN INVITE DAN ANYWAY? IT'S HIS WIFE I LIKE, SHE'S A SWEET GIRL. I MEAN, THESE ARE MY DOG PARK FRIENDS, OKAY? NOT MY REAL FRIENDS. MY REAL FRIENDS WOULDN'T...
I DON'T THINK THEY WOULD.
I DON'T KNOW.
OH, HONEY. I FEEL AWFUL.
YEAH. I KNOW.

I MEAN, WE'RE NOT A BUNCH OF YOKELS OVER HERE, FOR GOODNESS' SAKES! HALF MY FRIENDS HAVE KIDS WHO MARRIED, YOU KNOW...
PEOPLE OF COLOR?
IS THAT WHAT YOU SAY? WHAT A MOUTHFUL.
YES. AND YES.
I MEAN, IF YOU WANT TO TALK COLOR, I HAVE PLENTY, FRANKLY.
FROM A BOTTLE DOESN'T COUNT, MOM.
THAT'S WHAT YOU SAY.

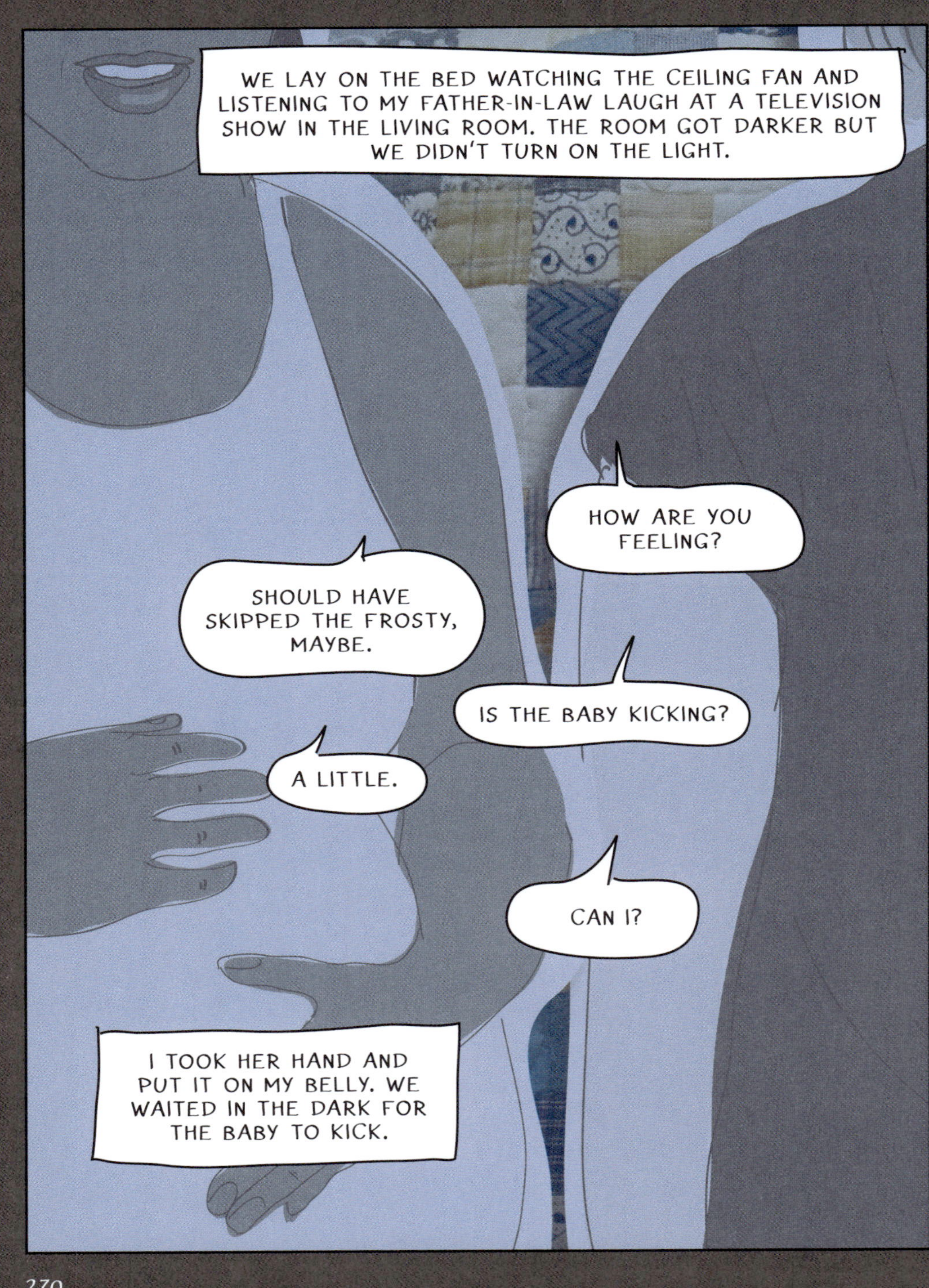
WE LAY ON THE BED WATCHING THE CEILING FAN AND LISTENING TO MY FATHER-IN-LAW LAUGH AT A TELEVISION SHOW IN THE LIVING ROOM. THE ROOM GOT DARKER BUT WE DIDN'T TURN ON THE LIGHT.
HOW ARE YOU FEELING?
SHOULD HAVE SKIPPED THE FROSTY, MAYBE.
IS THE BABY KICKING?
A LITTLE.
CAN I?
I TOOK HER HAND AND PUT IT ON MY BELLY. WE WAITED IN THE DARK FOR THE BABY TO KICK.

CHAPTER 32: A MORE PERFECT UNION

IN 2008, WE WATCHED A SENATOR FROM ILLINOIS RISE IN THE DEMOCRATIC PRIMARIES. HE WAS THE SON OF A BLACK, MUSLIM-BORN, KENYAN FATHER AND A WHITE KANSAN MOTHER, AND THOUGH ALL OF THOSE THINGS MADE HIM SOMEONE VERY SPECIFIC, THEY ALSO MADE HIM OURS. WE TOOK BETS ON WHAT WOULD BRING HIM DOWN, WHICH IS WHAT YOU DO WHEN YOU'RE TRYING TO BREAK YOUR OWN HEART BEFORE YOUR COUNTRY DOES IT FOR YOU.
I MEAN, WHAT IF HE TAKES THIS ALL THE—
SHHHHH!
THE POSSIBILITY WAS ALMOST TOO MUCH TO BEAR.

THEN IN MARCH THE VIDEOS SURFACED. ON THEM, THE SENATOR'S MINISTER CONDEMNED AMERICA'S LEGACY OF BLACK SLAVERY, NATIVE AMERICAN GENOCIDE, AND JAPANESE INTERNMENT.
NOT GOD BLESS AMERICA, GOD DAMN AMERICA!
THAT'S WHEN WE KNEW HOW IT WOULD END.
IT'S SO FUCKED. THEY MAKE THIS ENTIRE THING ABOUT RACE AND IF HE ADDRESSES IT DIRECTLY, HE'S THE ONE PLAYING THE RACE CARD.
YUP.

PUNDITS SAID HE WOULD WITHDRAW. A FEW DAYS LATER, I TURNED ON THE TELEVISION TO SEE IF HE HAD. HE WAS GIVING A SPEECH.
AT VARIOUS STAGES IN THE CAMPAIGN, SOME COMMENTATORS HAVE DEEMED ME EITHER "TOO BLACK" OR "NOT BLACK ENOUGH."
I CALLED JED AT WORK.
HEY, ARE YOU NEAR A TV?
BUT THE ANGER IS REAL; IT IS POWERFUL; AND TO SIMPLY WISH IT AWAY, TO CONDEMN IT WITHOUT UNDERSTANDING ITS ROOTS, ONLY SERVES TO WIDEN THE CHASM OF MISUNDERSTANDING THAT EXISTS BETWEEN THE RACES.

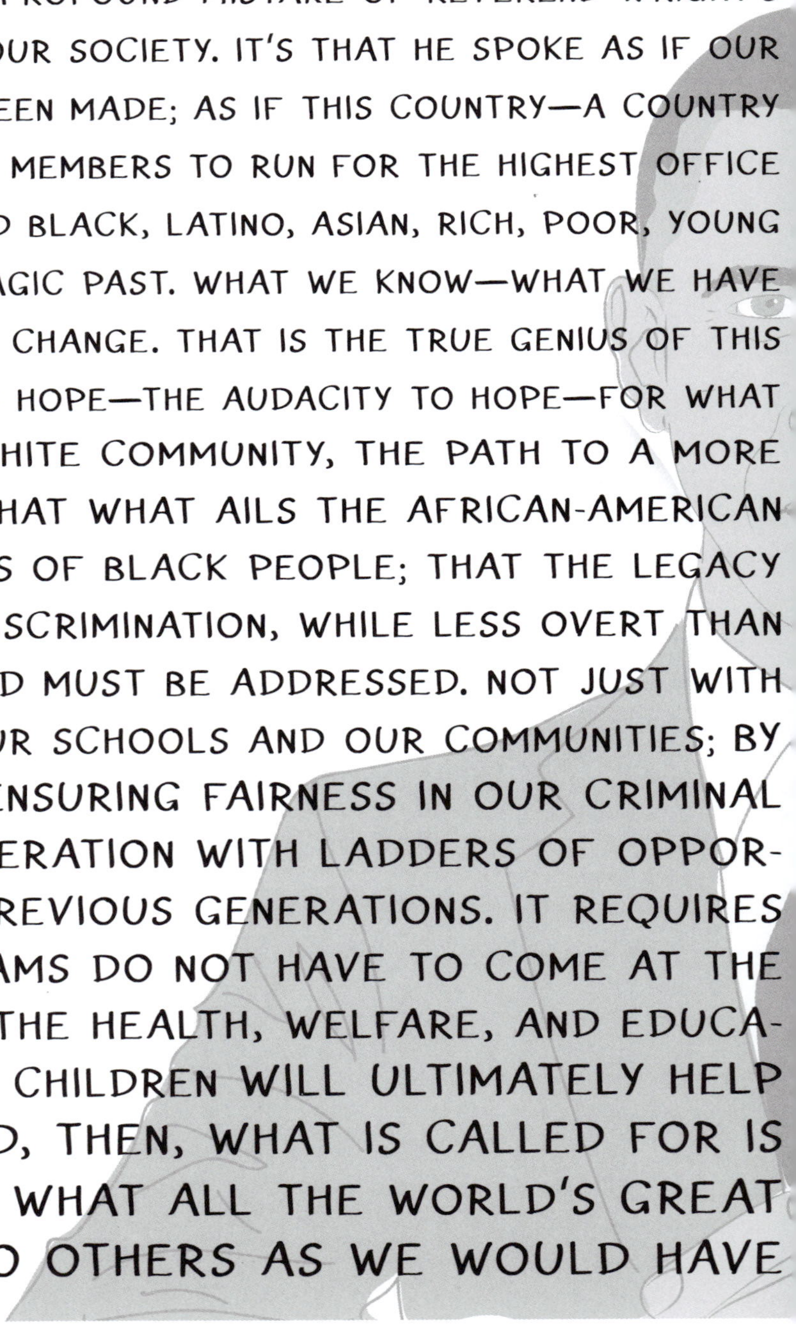

THE PROFOUND MISTAKE OF REVEREND WRIGHT'S
IN OUR SOCIETY. IT'S THAT HE SPOKE AS IF OUR
BEEN MADE; AS IF THIS COUNTRY—A COUNTRY
OWN MEMBERS TO RUN FOR THE HIGHEST OFFICE
AND BLACK, LATINO, ASIAN, RICH, POOR, YOUNG
TRAGIC PAST. WHAT WE KNOW—WHAT WE HAVE
CAN CHANGE. THAT IS THE TRUE GENIUS OF THIS
US HOPE—THE AUDACITY TO HOPE—FOR WHAT
THE WHITE COMMUNITY, THE PATH TO A MORE
THAT WHAT AILS THE AFRICAN-AMERICAN
MINDS OF BLACK PEOPLE; THAT THE LEGACY
OF DISCRIMINATION, WHILE LESS OVERT THAN
AND MUST BE ADDRESSED. NOT JUST WITH
OUR SCHOOLS AND OUR COMMUNITIES; BY
ENSURING FAIRNESS IN OUR CRIMINAL
GENERATION WITH LADDERS OF OPPOR-
PREVIOUS GENERATIONS. IT REQUIRES
DREAMS DO NOT HAVE TO COME AT THE
IN THE HEALTH, WELFARE, AND EDUCA-
CHILDREN WILL ULTIMATELY HELP
END, THEN, WHAT IS CALLED FOR IS
THAN WHAT ALL THE WORLD'S GREAT
UNTO OTHERS AS WE WOULD HAVE

SERMONS IS NOT THAT HE SPOKE ABOUT RACISM
SOCIETY WAS STATIC; AS IF NO PROGRESS HAD
THAT HAS MADE IT POSSIBLE FOR ONE OF HIS
IN THE LAND AND BUILD A COALITION OF WHITE
AND OLD—IS STILL IRREVOCABLY BOUND TO A
SEEN—IS THAT AMERICA CAN CHANGE. AMERICA
NATION. WHAT WE HAVE ALREADY ACHIEVED GIVES
WE CAN AND MUST ACHIEVE TOMORROW. NOW, IN
PERFECT UNION MEANS ACKNOWLEDGING
COMMUNITY DOES NOT JUST EXIST IN THE
OF DISCRIMINATION—AND CURRENT INCIDENTS
IN THE PAST—THAT THESE THINGS ARE REAL
WORDS, BUT WITH DEEDS—BY INVESTING IN
ENFORCING OUR CIVIL RIGHTS LAWS AND
JUSTICE SYSTEM; BY PROVIDING THIS
TUNITY THAT WERE UNAVAILABLE FOR
ALL AMERICANS TO REALIZE THAT YOUR
EXPENSE OF MY DREAMS; THAT INVESTING
TION OF BLACK AND BROWN AND WHITE
ALL OF AMERICA PROSPER. IN THE
NOTHING MORE AND NOTHING LESS
RELIGIONS DEMAND: THAT WE DO
THEM DO UNTO US.

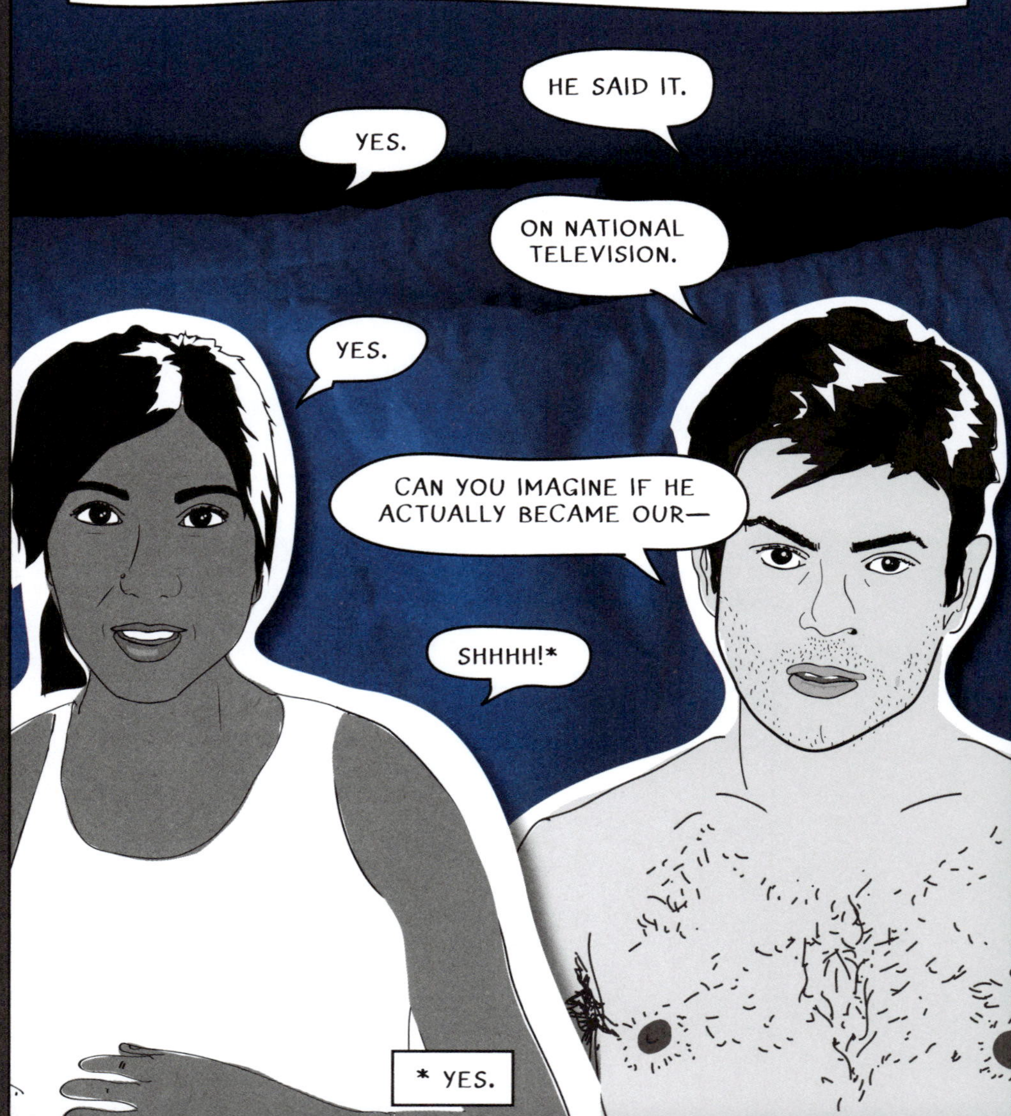
SOMETIMES, YOU HEAR SOMEONE SAY SOMETHING SO NEW AND TRUE AND OBVIOUS THAT IT COMPLETELY BEWILDERS YOU, MAKING THE FAMILIAR PATHS OF YOUR DAILY LIFE UNRECOGNIZABLE. HOW, YOU WONDER, DID YOU NOT SEE IT BEFORE, THIS PARTICULAR ROAD FORWARD, THIS WAY OF MOVING THAT NO LONGER REQUIRES YOU TO LEAD YOURSELF ASTRAY?
HE SAID IT.
YES.
ON NATIONAL TELEVISION.
YES.
CAN YOU IMAGINE IF HE ACTUALLY BECAME OUR—
SHHHH!*
* YES.

CHAPTER 33: LATE SEPTEMBER 2016

BY FALL, JED'S PARENTS DIDN'T CALL AS OFTEN, AND WHEN THEY DID, IT WAS STRAINED. MOSTLY I TRIED NOT TO TALK ABOUT ALL THE ANGRY WHITE FACES WE SAW ON THE TELEVISION, HOW WORRIED I WAS FOR Z, HOW BETRAYED I FELT BY THEM.
HI, DEAR. HOW IS EVERYONE DOING?
HI, MOM. PRETTY GOOD.
ANY PLANS THIS WEEKEND?
SOMETIMES, THOUGH, I JUST WANTED THEM TO KNOW.
ACTUALLY, THINGS ARE KIND OF WEIRD OVER HERE.
OH NO! WHAT HAPPENED?
ALL THIS TRUMP STUFF, THE WAY PEOPLE ARE TALKING ABOUT IMMIGRANTS, IT'S SCARING Z.
HE DOESN'T NEED TO BE AFRAID OF ANYTHING!

THAT'S NOT TRUE, THOUGH. WHEN PEOPLE GET ANGRY WITH BROWN PEOPLE, THEY DON'T REALLY DISTINGUISH, YOU KNOW? SO WHEN HE SEES ON THE NEWS THAT—
HE'S AN 8-YEAR-OLD CHILD! HE DOESN'T NEED TO BE WATCHING THE NEWS.
BUT IT'S NOT JUST THAT.
WHEN HE'S DOWN HERE WITH ME, WE WATCH CARTOONS.

WE CAN'T JUST IGNORE THIS STUFF, MOM.
LISTEN, DEAR, WE'RE ENTITLED TO VOTE THE WAY WE WANT TO. YOU DON'T AGREE WITH US, FINE. BUT I DON'T WANT TO DISCUSS IT ANYMORE.
IT'S JUST—
DAD GOT SO UPSET LAST TIME. YOU GUYS HAVE TO LET THIS GO. IT'S JUST NOT WORTH IT.

WHO ARE YOU TALKING TO?
GRANDMA.
I WANT TO TALK TO GRANDMA!
IS THAT Z? HI, SWEETHEART!!
HOLD ON, HE'S COMING.
HI, GRANDMA!

CHAPTER 34: EARLY OCTOBER 2016

WHAT? WHY?
BECAUSE WHEN HE FIRST STARTED ASKING ME QUESTIONS ABOUT ALL THIS, I THOUGHT I COULD ANSWER THEM. WHY DOES TRUMP SAY MEXICANS ARE RAPISTS? BECAUSE HE'S RACIST. WHY DID HE SAY THAT HE CAN GRAB A WOMAN BY HER—
LOCALS ONLY
OH MY GOD, NO.
Z SAID "PUSSY"?!
HE'S JUST REPEATING WHAT HE HEARS ON THE NEWS. CAN YOU IMAGINE FOUR MORE YEARS OF THIS?

HONESTLY I DON'T EVEN KNOW WHAT TO SAY ANYMORE. I DON'T UNDERSTAND WHAT IS HAPPENING, EITHER. THIS WHOLE TIME, I'VE BEEN ALL, "YES, THIS IS SCARY AND WEIRD, BUT DON'T WORRY, THE GOOD PEOPLE WILL SEE THIS FOR THIS UGLINESS IT IS. THEY WILL STAND UP FOR US AND WE'LL BE OKAY." I MEAN, WHAT DOES THAT EVEN MEAN? ARE THERE? WHERE ARE THEY, ALL THESE GOOD AMERICANS?

HOW ARE THINGS WITH YOUR IN-LAWS?
UGH.
THE SAME?
THEY DON'T WANT TO TALK ABOUT WHAT'S GOING ON, AND I DON'T KNOW WHAT ELSE THERE IS TO SAY. EVERY TIME THEY CALL I'M SCARED I'M GOING TO CRY OR START YELLING AT THEM. I TELL Z THEY LOVE HIM, I TELL JED WE'RE GOING TO FIND A WAY THROUGH, BUT BETWEEN US? I FEEL SICK ABOUT IT ALL THE TIME.
I DON'T KNOW HOW YOU DEAL WITH IT. I WOULD LOSE MY SHIT IF MY MAN'S MOM DID THAT.
I'M TRYING NOT TO MAKE IT WORSE FOR JED....
SPOOKY CIDER!

HOW IS HE HANDLING IT?
HE'S UPSET. HURT. HE WROTE THEM A LETTER SAYING, "THIS IS MY WIFE, MY CHILD. PLEASE CONSIDER HOW THIS WILL HARM OUR FAMILY."
AND?
THEY SAID THEY WERE SORRY HE FELT THAT WAY BUT THEY DIDN'T.
OH MAN. POOR JED.

I DON'T GET IT. I DON'T GET HOW YOU LISTEN TO THAT MAN SAY HATEFUL THINGS ABOUT PEOPLE WHO LOOK LIKE US AND PRETEND IT DOESN'T MEAN WHAT IT MEANS.
THEY'RE SLEEPWALKING.
WHAT?
SOMEONE—KIESE LAYMON I THINK—SAID MOST WHITE PEOPLE ARE SLEEPWALKING WHEN IT COMES TO RACISM IN AMERICA. THEY DON'T SEE IT SO THEY THINK IT DOESN'T EXIST ANYMORE. FORCING THEM TO SEE THAT IT IS HAPPENING HERE, NOW, IS LIKE WAKING UP A SLEEPWALKER. THEY GET DISORIENTED. ANGRY AT YOU INSTEAD OF ABOUT THE RACISM ITSELF.

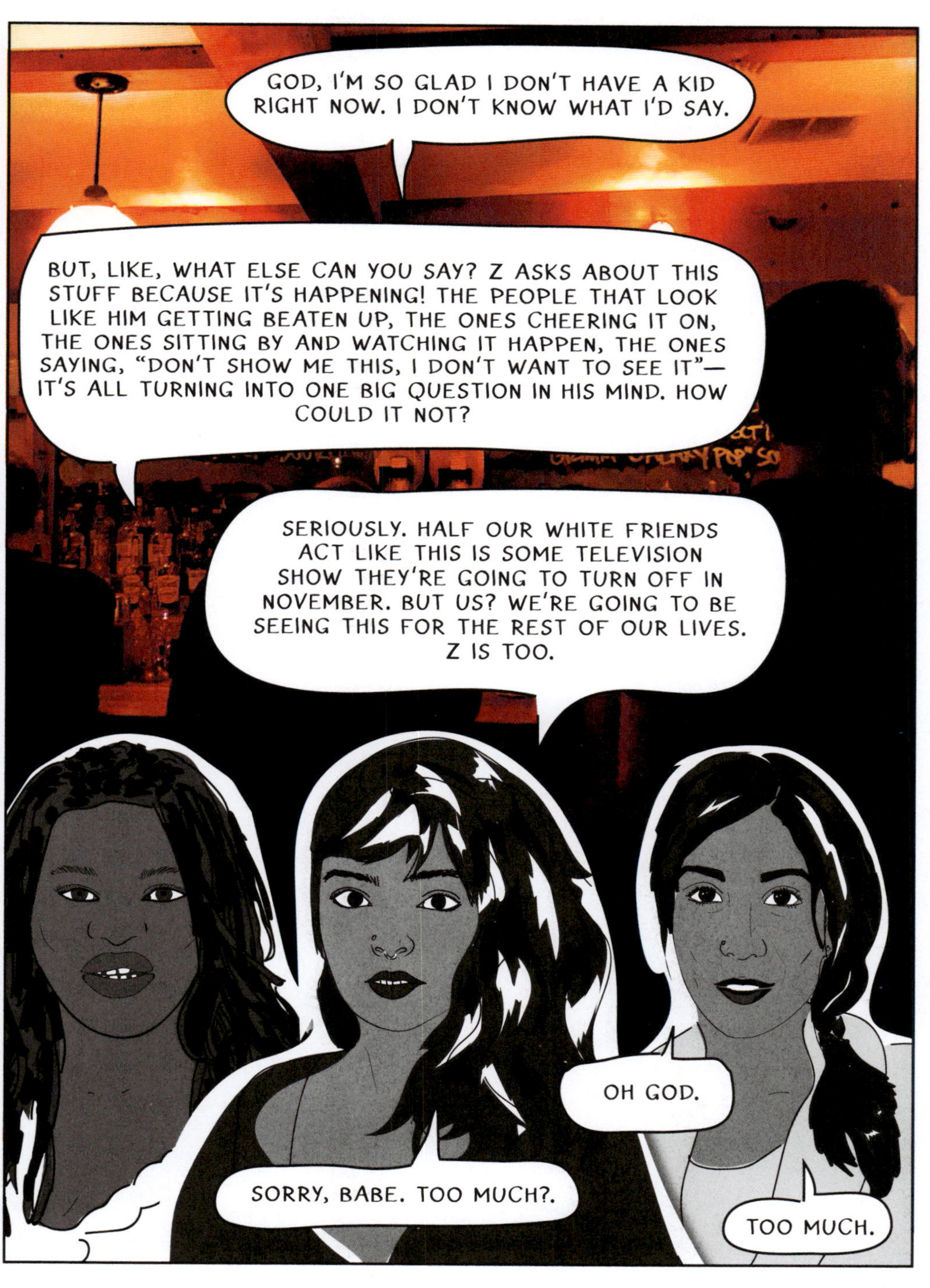
GOD, I'M SO GLAD I DON'T HAVE A KID RIGHT NOW. I DON'T KNOW WHAT I'D SAY.
BUT, LIKE, WHAT ELSE CAN YOU SAY? Z ASKS ABOUT THIS STUFF BECAUSE IT'S HAPPENING! THE PEOPLE THAT LOOK LIKE HIM GETTING BEATEN UP, THE ONES CHEERING IT ON, THE ONES SITTING BY AND WATCHING IT HAPPEN, THE ONES SAYING, "DON'T SHOW ME THIS, I DON'T WANT TO SEE IT"—IT'S ALL TURNING INTO ONE BIG QUESTION IN HIS MIND. HOW COULD IT NOT?
SERIOUSLY. HALF OUR WHITE FRIENDS ACT LIKE THIS IS SOME TELEVISION SHOW THEY'RE GOING TO TURN OFF IN NOVEMBER. BUT US? WE'RE GOING TO BE SEEING THIS FOR THE REST OF OUR LIVES. Z IS TOO.
OH GOD.
SORRY, BABE. TOO MUCH?.
TOO MUCH.

CHAPTER 35: MID-OCTOBER 2016

WHAT DID YOU TELL HIM?

THE TRUTH. THAT THEY LOVE HIM. THAT THEY LOVE YOU. THAT THEIR POLITICS DON'T CHANGE THAT.

THEY LOVE YOU, TOO, YOU KNOW.

YOU THINK THEY'D FEEL THE SAME ABOUT ME IF I VOTED FOR AN ANTI-SEMITE?
THEY DON'T SEE IT THAT WAY.
BUT IT IS THAT WAY.

I DON'T KNOW THAT IT'S HELPFUL TO BE SO BLACK-AND-WHITE ABOUT IT.
RIGHT.
LOOK, I'M NOT DEFENDING THEM. I DON'T AGREE WITH THEM. BUT IF WE'RE GOING TO STAY IN A PLACE WHERE WE CAN STILL COMMUNICATE EFFECTIVELY WITH THEM—
IS THIS US COMMUNICATING EFFECTIVELY WITH THEM?
THIS IS ME TRYING TO STAY IN A PLACE WHERE I STILL CAN.

I JUST...I ALWAYS THOUGHT THEY WOULD CHOOSE FAMILY FIRST. OVER EVERYTHING. I MEAN, I KNOW WE'RE REALLY DIFFERENT, OKAY? BUT I THOUGHT WE WERE CLOSE DESPITE THAT. I WAS PROUD OF THAT, EVEN. AND NOW I JUST FEEL LIKE I WAS WRONG ABOUT EVERYTHING.
EVERYTHING? COME ON.
LOOK, I DON'T GET IT, EITHER. I DON'T KNOW HOW PEOPLE GO FROM BEING LIBERTARIANS TO HOLDING SIGNS ON STREET CORNERS FOR THIS GUY, OKAY? BUT THAT DOESN'T MEAN YOUR ENTIRE 15-YEAR RELATIONSHIP WITH THEM IS SUDDENLY—
THEY ARE HOLDING SIGNS FOR HIM?!

I'M JUST SAYING—
STOP JUST SAYING! DON'T SAY ANYTHING! WHAT WOULD YOU DO?! IF IT WERE MY CHRISTIAN PARENTS, SAYING, "LOOK, JED, JEWISH PEOPLE ARE SAYING THE GUY HATES JEWS BUT WE JUST DON'T SEE IT, SO WE'RE GOING TO GO OUT THERE AND *HOLD SIGNS* SUPPORTING HIM!" HOW WOULD YOU FEEL IN THEIR HOME?
I...
I WOULD FEEL AWFUL.
I FEEL AWFUL.
I FEEL LIKE THEY'VE ABANDONED ME.

CHAPTER 36: BOOK BUSINESS

I WROTE MY FIRST NOVEL EVERY NIGHT FROM 11 P.M. TO 1 A.M. IT TOOK ME 10 YEARS TO FINISH IT. WHEN IT SOLD A FEW WEEKS LATER, I WAS IN SHOCK.
OH MY GOD, MOM, MY BOOK IS GOING TO BE PUBLISHED!
THAT IS SO WONDERFUL!!! HOW MUCH DID YOU SELL IT FOR???
WAIT, WHAT??? CAN'T WE JUST BE HAPPY FOR A MOMENT WITHOUT TALKING ABOUT THAT?
YES!!! I AM SO HAPPY!!!
BUT YOUR GRANDMOTHER WILL WANT TO KNOW.

IN THE SUMMER OF 2015, A PUBLIC RADIO PRODUCER FROM BOSTON CALLED. HE WANTED ME TO READ A SEGMENT OF IT ON AIR FOR HIS SHOW. I WAS EXCITED.

THAT'S GREAT, SWEETIE.

I SHOULD DO IT, RIGHT?

FOR SURE.

GROWING UP IN NEW MEXICO, I LISTENED TO NPR EVERY DAY. IT FELT LIKE LISTENING TO LIFE ON A PLANET I'D NEVER GET TO.

WHY WOULDN'T YOU DO IT?

THE PRODUCER ASKED ME TO CHOOSE A FEW EXCERPTS AND SEND THEM TO HIM SO HE COULD EDIT. A FEW DAYS LATER, THE EDITS CAME BACK.

Dear Mira,

Please see attached edits. We do triple back flips to make all our passages totally comprehensible. Having three characters with unusual names is confusing. It would be better with two. Would a teenager really say "mark my words"? Maybe. Please write an introductory couple sentences to set up the scene to fully orient listeners and then pass it back to us.

—Boston Radio Producer

I HAD BEEN ON A BOOK TOUR EARLIER IN THE YEAR, SO IN TERMS OF WEIRD ASKS PEOPLE HAD ABOUT THE BOOK, THIS WAS PRETTY LOW.
HOW MUCH OF AN EDGE WOULD YOU SAY YOUR DIVERSITY GAVE WITH PUBLISHERS?
YOUR PARENTS MUST BE FEELING SO EMBARRASSED, NO?
IS THERE A RESTAURANT NEARBY YOU CONSIDER AUTHENTIC?
MY SON IS DATING AN INDIAN WOMAN?

BUT I WAS CONFUSED.
DID YOU TELL HIM THE BOOK HAS ALREADY BEEN PUBLISHED IN 11 COUNTRIES WITH THE UNUSUAL NAMES?
I MEAN, AM I SUPPOSED TO CUT A CHARACTER? CHANGE ALL OF THEIR NAMES?
NO! COME ON. YOU'RE THE CREATOR. YOU'RE SUPPOSED TO PROTECT YOUR WORK AGAINST BAD EDITS.
MAYBE I SHOULD SUBMIT ANOTHER SCENE.
THE ONE WITHOUT ANY INDIANS IN IT?
THEY ALL HAVE INDIANS IN THEM!
MIRA.
OH. HA.

THE NEXT DAY, I TOLD MYSELF ANY PUBLICITY WAS GOOD PUBLICITY. I TOLD MYSELF I WAS LUCKY TO EVEN HAVE THIS PROBLEM AT ALL. I WROTE BACK.

Dear Boston Radio Producer,

Thanks for the edits. I fixed some grammatical errors. To your question—yes, this teen speaks that way. Hopefully, his distinct voice will make having three characters less confusing.

For intro, how about: It's 1983 in Corrales, New Mexico. Amina, Akhil, and Dimple, three East Indian teenagers, sit on a roof, waiting for the annual migration of the snow geese.

THAT AFTERNOON, HE WROTE BACK.

Thanks, Mira.

Of course, any edits we do are approved by you, the creator, and we want to honor your creation. I'm your radio adviser and just wanted to make suggestions. We're a team to make a great teaser for your book.

For intro, let's try: It's the year 1983 in Corrales, New Mexico. Three Asian Indian teenagers are up on their family's roof. They're waiting for the annual migration of majestic snow geese!

—Boston Radio Producer

I CALLED SOME FRIENDS.
HEY, HAVE YOU EVER CALLED YOURSELF ASIAN INDIAN?
NO.
NOPE.
YES, WHEN I WAS LOBOTOMIZED. OOPS, JUST KIDDING—NOT EVEN THEN.
I'M BANGLA, BITCH.

I CALLED JED AT WORK.
WAIT, WHAT'S THE PROBLEM?
"ASIAN INDIAN" IS JUST, LIKE...COLONIAL OR SOMETHNG. LIKE, LET'S SAY YOU HAD TO INTRODUCE YOURSELF AS A CAUCASIAN JEW. THAT WOULD BE WEIRD, RIGHT?
I JUST THINK YOU HAVE TO PICK YOUR BATTLES HERE.
I KNOW, BUT—
I MEAN, WHAT DO YOU WANT TO DO, WRITE HIM SOME LONG EXPLA-NATION? HE DOESN'T KNOW THIS STUFF. FINE. JUST CORRECT HIM AND MOVE ON.
I KNOW, I KNOW.

I WROTE THE EMAIL FAST SO I WOULDN'T OVERTHINK IT.

Looks good—small fix below.

It's the year 1983 in Corrales, New Mexico. Three East Indian teenagers are up on their family's roof. They're waiting for the annual migration of majestic snow geese!

THE EMAIL BACK CAME SURPRISINGLY FAST.

Mira,

Since New Mexico for a lot of people = American Indians, and Americans (alas!) are not used to the term "East Indians," and then there are, for further confusion, "West Indians," we are suggesting merely going with Asian Indians for the purposes of this short radio piece, for full clarity. We hope this clears it up for you.

Thanks,
Boston Radio Producer

HE THINKS I'M NOT AMERICAN.
WHAT? WHO?
THE RADIO PRODUCER.
HE THINKS YOU'RE—
HE IS TELLING ME WHAT AMERICANS THINK BECAUSE HE THINKS I'M NOT ONE MYSELF.
HONEY, YOU'RE SHOUTING.
IT HAS BEEN A LONG YEAR. NO, FUCK THAT—IT HAS BEEN A LONG LIFE.
CAN YOU CALM DOWN AND WRITE HIM?
YES.

I DID NOT CALM DOWN. I TOOK A SHOT OF WHISKEY. I WROTE:

Dear Boston Radio Producer,

Wait a minute. Just hold on. Are you really telling me that there are people in the world called...*West Indians*? Good god! What else can you tell me? Are there a lot of them? How many have unusual names? Do you think they'd be cool with calling themselves East of Mexico/South of Florida Indians instead, for full clarity?
all best,

Mira

P.S. Possible intro change, in light of this:

"Don't be fooled by the unusual names you're about to hear; this is just a story about human beings."

I IMAGINED HITTING SEND. I IMAGINED NO ONE EVER PUBLISHING ANYTHING BY ME AGAIN. I DELETED THE EMAIL AND WROTE:

Dear Boston Radio Producer,

Totally understand your need for clarity in intro. Alas, I am American. I was born and raised here. Asian Indian is just not a term used to describe us. If confusing, let's use South Asian. See you next week.

MJ

THEN I CALLED ALISON.

A LOT OF TIMES WHEN I DON'T UNDERSTAND A SITUATION WITH A WHITE PERSON, I WILL ASK ALISON ABOUT IT, WHICH IS BOTH LAZY AND SUPER HELPFUL.
I'VE BEEN MEANING TO CALL YOU OUT ON THAT.
PLEASE DON'T.
WHAT A DUMBASS.
WHY DO I FEEL BETTER WHEN YOU GET MAD?
HOW DO GUYS LIKE THIS KEEP THEIR JOBS? THAT IS WHAT I WANT TO KNOW.
IT'S LIKE A FULL-BODY MASSAGE.
I MEAN, LISTEN, IT'S NOT THAT I'M NOT THANKFUL. I AM THANKFUL.
YOU'RE SUPPOSED TO BE THANKFUL ABOUT THIS?

I'M SUPPOSED TO BE THANKFUL FOR EVERYTHING. THANK YOU FOR PUBLISHING ME! THANK YOU FOR ASKING ME TO ATTEND AN EVENT! THANK YOU FOR THANKING ME FOR WRITING CHARACTERS YOU COULD RELATE TO DESPITE THEM BEING INDIAN! THANK YOU FOR SAYING YOU ALMOST FELT LIKE THEY WERE JUST NORMAL PEOPLE!

OH GOD, THAT GUY.

THANK YOU FOR TELLING ME YOU WISH YOU HAD BEEN BRAVE ENOUGH TO DATE THE INDIAN GIRLS IN YOUR HIGH SCHOOL! THANK YOU FOR ASKING ME ABOUT WHETHER OR NOT YOU SHOULD TAKE A VACATION TO INDIA! THANK YOU FOR TELLING ME THAT YOUR INDIAN NEIGHBOR MAKES YOUR HALLWAY SMELL LIKE CURRY! THANK YOU FOR TELLING ME YOU HATE CURRY! THANK YOU FOR APOLOGIZING FOR HATING CURRY, LIKE I AM CURRY'S MOTHER!

I JUST...I ALWAYS TOLD MYSELF THAT BY THE TIME I GOT OLDER, IT WOULDN'T BE LIKE THIS ANYMORE. BUT EVERY DOOR I GET THROUGH, THIS GUY IS ALWAYS ON THE OTHER SIDE. PATTING HIMSELF ON THE BACK FOR BEING OPEN-MINDED WHILE MAKING SURE I SCRUB MYSELF BEFORE I ENTER. IT MAKES ME FEEL CRAZY.
THAT WOULD MAKE ANYONE FEEL CRAZY.
YOU?
WOULD I FEEL CRAZY?
YEAH.
WAIT. YOU THINK YOU FEEL BAD BECAUSE SOMETHING IS WRONG WITH YOU?

ONE OF THE REASONS I LOVE ALISON IS BECAUSE SHE DOES NOT PANIC IF I SUDDENLY START CRYING.
I DON'T EVEN KNOW WHY I'M—
I MEAN, WHY IS THIS EVEN A BIG DEAL? IT'S NOT. SO MUCH WORSE HAS HAPPENED.
BUT SOMETHING IS HAPPENING. I CAN'T EXPLAIN IT. HALF OF MY FRIENDS ARE HUDDLED, WAITING FOR IT TO HIT, AND THE OTHER HALF ARE LIKE, "WHY DOES EVERYTHING HAVE TO BE POLITICAL? WHERE IS THIS COMING FROM?" I WANT TO YELL, "DON'T YOU FUCKING FEEL IT? HOW CAN YOU NOT FEEL IT?"
AND THEN THESE LITTLE THINGS, THESE THINGS I SHOULD PROBABLY JUST IGNORE BECAUSE I'VE BEEN IGNORING THEM MY WHOLE LIFE, THEY FEEL LIKE THE ONLY WAY TO FIGHT BACK BECAUSE IF I DON'T ALL THE BIGGER SHIT WILL CRUSH US.
UGH.

THEY DON'T.
WHAT?
WHITE PEOPLE. FEEL IT. I MEAN, I DON'T THINK THEY DO. NOT TO SPEAK FOR ALL WHITE PEOPLE OR ANYTHING.
OH.
WAIT, YOU CAN'T DO THAT? SPEAK FOR ALL OF YOU?
I MEAN, WE HAD THAT CONFERENCE CALL THIS MORNING, BUT YOU KNOW HOW IT IS.

THE MORNING I WAS SUPPOSED TO GO RECORD WITH THE BOSTON RADIO PRODUCER, I TRIED ON EVERYTHING IN MY CLOSET. NOTHING WORKED.
YOU LOOK NICE, SWEETIE.
TOO FOREIGNER.
WHAT?
IF I LOOK TOO FORMAL, HE'LL THINK I'M A FOREIGNER AND TALK DOWN TO ME THAT WAY, BUT IF I WEAR JEANS AND A T-SHIRT, HE'LL DO THE OLDER-GUY/ YOUNGER-WOMAN THING.
HUH?
NEEDS TO BE PERFECT.

WAIT, THIS IS FOR THAT ASSHOLE PRODUCER GUY?!

IF I WEAR THE RIGHT CLOTHES, IT WILL GO BETTER.

MIRA.

WHAT?

THIS IS INSANE.

FORGET THIS GUY. HE'S AN IDIOT. YOU WROTE A GREAT BOOK, END OF STORY.
BUT THAT'S NOT WHAT I'M—
WHAT HE THINKS DOESN'T MATTER.
JED, I'M NOT—
YOU DON'T HAVE TO WEAR SOME KIND OF PERFECT OUTFIT INTO A RECORDING SESSION TO CONVINCE HIM YOU ARE GOOD ENOUGH! FOR WHAT, HIS STUPID RADIO SHOW? SCREW HIM! YOU ARE GREAT!
GET OUT.

WHAT?

NOW.

WHAT ARE YOU—

GET THE FUCK OUT OF THIS ROOM RIGHT NOW.

I'M SORRY. I SHOULDN'T HAVE SNAPPED.

WHAT THE HELL?

BUT I'M NOT CRAZY.

I NEVER SAID YOU WERE.

YOU DON'T GET IT.

I WAS JUST SAYING—

YOU WERE ACTING LIKE I JUST NEEDED TO FEEL BETTER ABOUT MYSELF OR CONFIDENT OR SOMETHING—

BECAUSE THAT GUY IS JUST SOME ASSHOLE AND—

PLEASE STOP TALKING.

DO YOU KNOW HOW MUCH I USED TO COPY YOU?
WHAT?
IT'S TRUE. IN OUR 20s, I WATCHED YOU WALK INTO ROOMS AND I WOULD THINK, WHAT IS THAT? I WANT THAT. AND WHEN YOU WEREN'T AROUND, I WOULD PUT IT ON LIKE A COSTUME. I WOULD WALK INTO WORK AND TALK LIKE SOMEONE EVERYONE KNOWS THEY NEED TO PAY ATTENTION TO. IT WAS A DECENT STRATEGY. SOMETIMES IT MADE MY BOSSES TRY TO SLEEP WITH ME, BUT SOMETIMES IT ACTUALLY WORKED.
BUT IT'S 20 YEARS LATER. THE ROOMS ARE HARDER TO GET INTO. AND YOU KNOW WHO MEN LIKE THIS GUY DON'T WANT IN THEM?
MIRA—
ME.

THAT'S NOT TRUE.
IT IS MORE TRUE THAN YOU THINK. IT'S MORE TRUE THAN I TELL YOU ABOUT. AND YOU ARE RIGHT, BY THE WAY, IT IS NOT MY FAULT. IT ISN'T ABOUT ME NOT BEING GOOD OR CONFIDENT ENOUGH. BUT YOU KNOW WHAT I'M NOT?
I AM NOT THE ENEMY.
I AM NOT A WHITE MAN.

YOU TALK LIKE I'M SOME GUY FROM THE '50s WHO HAS NEVER THOUGHT ABOUT THIS BEFORE.
I TALK TO YOU LIKE SOMEONE WHO DOESN'T THINK ABOUT IT BECAUSE YOU HAVEN'T HAD TO. LIKE YOU'RE SOMEONE WHO JUST TOLD ME TO BE *CONFIDENT*.
JESUS CHRIST, I WAS TRYING TO HELP. THIS GUY SUCKS AND YOU'RE LETTING HIM DERAIL YOU!
THIS GUY IS **MY WHOLE LIFE!** ME FIGURING HOW TO GET PAST THIS GUY IS ALL I EVER DO! YOU THINK THIS IS DERAILING? SHUT UP.

WHERE ARE YOU GOING? I'M TALKING TO YOU!
NO, YOU'RE SHOUTING AT ME AND TELLING ME TO SHUT UP AND I'VE GOT TO GET TO WORK.
YOU ARE NOT ALLOWED TO BE BLIND ABOUT THIS! NOT WHEN YOU MARRIED ME!
WHAT?
YOU DON'T GET TO KNOW THIS LITTLE ABOUT WHAT IT IS LIKE! NOT WHEN OUR SON LOOKS LIKE ME!
ABOUT WHAT WHAT IS LIKE? YOUR LIFE? Z'S?

YOU THINK I DON'T KNOW YOU GUYS?
MIRA?

CHAPTER 37: OCTOBER 31, 2016

ANOTHER DONALD TRUMP! WE'VE SEEN THREE TONIGHT ALREADY!
OH YEAH?
YES. ZOMBIE DONALD TRUMP, VAMPIRE DONALD TRUMP, AND DONALD VOLDEMORT TRUMP.
HELLO, BROOKLYN!
ARE GRANDMA AND GRAMPA STILL VOTING FOR HIM?
LAST I HEARD, YES.

MAYBE THEY CHANGED THEIR MINDS ABOUT IT.
MAYBE.
MAYBE WE SHOULD CALL AND ASK THEM TO PLEASE—
NOPE.
BUT IF WE BEG THEM—
ABSOLUTELY NOT.
BECAUSE YOU GUYS AREN'T TALKING ANYMORE?

SWEETHEART, I NEED TO TELL YOU SOMETHING, A KIND OF GROWN-UP THING. YOUR GRANDPARENTS AREN'T GOING TO CHANGE THEIR MINDS ABOUT THIS. IT'S JUST NOT GOING TO HAPPEN, AND I DON'T WANT YOU ASKING THEM TO DO THAT, OKAY?
BUT AREN'T THEY SCARED THAT TRUMP IS RACIST?
I DON'T THINK THEY THINK OF HIM THAT WAY.
SO HE'S NOT RACIST?
NO, HE IS, BUT I DON'T THINK THEY'RE REALLY LOOKING AT THAT PART.
AND WE ARE STILL TALKING, BY THE WAY, JUST LESS OFTEN.
AND THEY STILL LOVE YOU.

YOU OKAY?
I'M SAD.
YEAH. IT'S OKAY TO FEEL SAD. I'M SAD TOO.

CHAPTER 38: HOW IT HAPPENED

AND I HAD A MOHAWK!
HIGH AND FIERCE. GRANDMA TRIED TO COMB IT DOWN BUT IT WOULDN'T STAY. IT MADE US LAUGH.
AND AMMA?
AMMA HELD YOU FOR HOURS. SHE WAS SO MUCH MORE EXCITED ABOUT YOU THAN SHE EVER WAS ABOUT ME OR UNCLE ARUN.
REALLY?
DEFINITELY.
TUES

AND THEN OBAMA GOT ELECTED!

HE DID! WE HAD ALL OUR FRIENDS OVER TO WATCH THE ELECTION RESULTS AND WE TOOK TURNS HOLDING YOU.

DID YOU KNOW HE WOULD WIN?

YOU KNOW WHAT'S FUNNY? I WENT UP AND DOWN PHILLY WITH FLYERS FOR HIM, KNOWING HE DESERVED IT MORE THAN ANYONE, BUT STILL DIDN'T THINK HE WOULD UNTIL HE DID.

WHY NOT?

I GUESS BY THAT POINT I WAS JUST SO USED TO THE BEST PERSON NOT WINNING IF HE...

HE WHAT?

NOTHING.

AND THEN WHAT HAPPENED?

THEN WE CRIED. WE CRIED AND CRIED AND CRIED.

ALL OF YOU?

EVERYONE. YOU EVER HEAR THE EXPRESSION "I HAD TO PINCH MYSELF TO BELIEVE IT"?

YEAH.

THAT IS A REAL, TRUE THING THAT HAPPENS. SOMETIMES YOUR BRAIN IS SO SURPRISED BY SOMETHING IT FEELS LIKE YOU MUST NOT EVEN BE YOU ANYMORE.

YOU'RE WEIRD, MOMMY.

DID DADDY CRY?

YES.

DADDY NEVER CRIES!

THAT'S TRUE.

BUT HE CRIED FOR OBAMA?

HE CRIED FOR YOU. HE CRIED BECAUSE OUR NEW PRESIDENT WAS MIXED-RACE JUST LIKE YOU, AND AMERICA BELIEVED IN HIM, AND SUDDENLY THERE WAS A NEW PLACE FOR YOU IN THE WORLD.

AND THEN EVERYONE DANCED!
WE RAN DOWN TO THE STREET WITH YOU AND EVERYONE ON OUR BLOCK WAS YELLING AND YOU COULD HEAR THE CARS HONKING ALL OVER ATLANTIC AND FLATBUSH.
WAS I YELLING?
NO! YOU WERE ASLEEP. YOU WERE JUST A LITTLE BABY.
I THINK I REMEMBER IT.
YEAH?
YEAH. I REMEMBER EVERYONE AND ALSO THE FIREWORKS.
THERE WERE FIREWORKS?
YES. THEY WERE ALL OVER THE SKY, ALL OVER THE WHOLE CITY. BOOM, BOOM, BOOM! I REMEMBER.

The New York Times
OBAMA
RACIAL BARRIER FALLS IN DECISIVE VICTORY

CHAPTER 39: NOVEMBER 8, 2016

EVERYONE IS SO SAD OUT THERE.
YOU SHOULD SLEEP.
I THINK KAITLYN AND TANWI WERE CRYING IN THE KITCHEN.
IF THE PRESIDENT DOESN'T LIKE US DOES THAT MEAN THE ARMY DOESN'T LIKE US?
WHAT IF THEY ONLY LIKE DADDY? WILL HE HAVE TO GIVE US UP?
THAT'S NOT GOING TO HAPPEN.
YOU SAID HE WOULDN'T WIN.
SHHHH. SHUT YOUR EYES NOW.

CHAPTER 40: DECEMBER 2016

WELL, I TELL YOU ONE THING: I AM NOT STOP-PING. I AM GOING TO ALL THE MARCHES. EVERY SINGLE ONE. THIS GOVERNMENT IS GOING TO HEAR FROM ME!
SHOCKER.
YOU KNOW WHAT MY FRIEND BARB SAID? SHE SAID, "SHIREEN, YOU ARE ALWAYS TRYING TO CHANGE THIS COUNTRY, BUT THIS COUNTRY TOOK YOUR FAMILY IN! YOU SHOULD BE GRATEFUL!"
BARB SAID THAT?!

AND I SAID, "BARBARA, YOU LISTEN TO ME: THIS COUNTRY IS *LUCKY* TO HAVE GOTTEN MY HUSBAND AND CHILDREN. THEY HAVE HELPED MAKE THIS COUNTRY GREAT AND DON'T YOU EVER FORGET IT."
AWW. WAIT, WHAT ABOUT YOU?
I'M NOT SO GREAT. BUT YOU GUYS ARE SOMETHING ELSE.
MOM.

CHAPTER 41: MARCH 2017

IS IT GOING TO BE WEIRD?
WHAT?
NO.
IS IT?
I MEAN, MAYBE.
I DON'T KNOW.
YES.

YES, IT WILL BE A LITTLE WEIRD. BUT ALSO, WE'RE A FAMILY, SO THIS IS JUST WHAT WE DO.
OKAY.

HOW ARE YOU DOING?
FINE.
HOW ARE YOU REALLY?
I HAVE NO IDEA.
YOU DIDN'T HAVE TO COME. I MEANT IT WHEN I SAID—
I KNOW.
THEY'RE LUCKY TO HAVE YOU.
I'M NOT DOING IT FOR THEM. I'M DOING IT FOR HIM AND FOR YOU.

SHOULD WE HAVE, LIKE, A SAFE WORD?
YOU KNOW, SOMETHING YOU SAY WHEN YOU NEED OUT FAST? SOMETHING ONLY I WOULD UNDERSTAND?
WHAT?
SERIOUSLY?
OR LIKE A GESTURE. A SIGNAL?
WHAT KIND OF SIGNAL?

WHAT IF YOU SET FIRE TO A GOLF COURSE AND THEN STAND SCREAMING "DIE, FLORIDA" IN FRONT OF IT?
OH, FOR SURE.
IS THAT SUBTLE ENOUGH?
MAYBE WE SHOULD DO THE CODE PHRASE.
HOW ABOUT "HONEY, CAN YOU HELP ME IN THE KITCHEN? MY SOUL CAN'T STOP WEEPING FOR THE DEATH OF HUMANITY"?
JED.
COME ON. THAT COULD MEAN ANYTHING.

I LIED.
WHAT?
I AM GOING FOR ALL OF US.
I KNOW.

CHAPTER 42: THE TALK WE HAVEN'T HAD

ONCE, BEFORE I HAD YOU, I SAW YOU. I KNOW IT SOUNDS CRAZY, BUT IT'S TRUE. I WAS PREGNANT AND STANDING ALONE OUTSIDE A PARTY, AND WHEN YOU KICKED, I SHUT MY EYES AND SAW YOU ON A BEACH WE WOULD ARRIVE AT ALMOST FIVE YEARS LATER. YOU WERE FACING THE WATER AND WEARING YOUR BLUE SWIMSUIT AND I KNEW, FROM THE CURVE IN YOUR SPINE AND THE NUT BROWN OF YOUR SKIN, THAT YOU WERE MINE TO PROTECT LIKE NOTHING ELSE EVER WILL BE.
SO WHEN YOU FIRST STARTED ASKING ME HARD QUESTIONS, THE ONES ABOUT AMERICA AND YOUR PLACE HERE, I WANTED TO FIND YOU THE RIGHT ANSWERS—THE KIND THAT WOULD MAKE YOU FEEL GOOD, WELCOME, AND LOVED. I THOUGHT IF I COULD JUST REMEMBER THE COUNTRY I'D BEEN RAISED TO BELIEVE IN, THE ONE I WAS SURE I WOULD EVENTUALLY GET TO, I'D BE ABLE TO GET US BACK THERE.
(*THAT DOESN'T EVEN MAKE SENSE*, YOU'D PROBABLY SAY IF I TOLD YOU THIS. *YOU CAN'T GET BACK TO SOMEWHERE YOU'VE NEVER BEEN*. AND YOU'D BE RIGHT.)

HERE IS THE THING, THOUGH, THE REAL, TRUE THING I STILL HAVE TROUBLE ADMITTING: I CAN'T PROTECT YOU FROM EVERYTHING. I CAN'T PROTECT YOU FROM BECOMING A BROWN MAN IN AMERICA. I CAN'T PROTECT YOU FROM SPENDING A LIFETIME CAUGHT BETWEEN THE BEAUTIFUL DREAM OF A DIVERSE NATION AND THE COMPLICATED REALITY OF ONE. I CAN'T EVEN PROTECT YOU FROM THE SIMPLE FACT THAT SOMETIMES, THE PEOPLE WHO LOVE US WILL CHOOSE A WORLD THAT DOESN'T.

EVEN NOW, JUST WRITING THAT DOWN, I WANT TO SAY SOMETHING THAT WILL MAKE IT OKAY, OR EVEN MAKE IT MAKE SENSE, BUT I CAN'T. WILL THEY EVER REALLY UNDERSTAND IT THEMSELVES? WILL THEY EVER CHANGE? I HAVE NO IDEA. OUR BURDEN IS HOW MUCH WE MIGHT LOVE THEM ANYWAY.

AND THIS IS MAYBE THE PART I WORRY ABOUT MOST, HOW THE WEIGHT OF THAT WILL TWIST YOU INTO SOMEONE YOU DON'T WANT TO BE, OR WORSE, MAKE YOU ASHAMED OF YOUR OWN HEART. I HOPE YOU WILL REMEMBER THAT YOU HAVE NOTHING TO BE ASHAMED OF. I HOPE YOU WILL REMEMBER THAT YOUR HEART IS A GOOD ONE, AND THAT YOUR CAPACITY TO FEEL LOVE, IN ALL ITS COMPLEXITY, IS A GIFT.

SOMETIMES, WHEN I'M FEELING LOW, OR OVERWHELMED, OR UNSURE, I REMIND MYSELF THAT THERE IS A YOU, AND YOU MIGHT ONE DAY BE A MAN WHO KEEPS ASKING SO MANY, MANY, MANY, MANY, QUESTIONS. (YOU WOULD SNORT AT THIS. YOU WOULD YELL, *LIES! YOU WOULD NOT LIKE THAT AT ALL!* BUT YOU'D BE WRONG.) BECAUSE IF YOU GROW UP TO BE THE KIND OF PERSON WHO ASKS QUESTIONS ABOUT WHO YOU ARE, WHY THINGS ARE THE WAY THEY ARE, AND WHAT WE COULD DO TO MAKE THEM BETTER, THEN YOU STILL HAVE HOPE FOR THIS WORLD. AND IF YOU STILL HAVE HOPE, MY LOVE, THEN SO DO I.

ENORMOUS THANKS TO:

MY HUSBAND, JED ROTHSTEIN, WHO SAID, "JUST WRITE THE TRUTH AND WE'LL GO FROM THERE." ALISON HART, WHO SAID, "DO YOU WANT TO TALK ABOUT IT?" AND THEN HELPED ME MAKE SENSE OF WHAT CAME OUT. KAITLYN GREENIDGE AND TANWI ISLAM, WHO KEPT TELLING ME, "WRITE FOR US." MY MOTHER AND BROTHER, SHIREEN AND ARUN JACOB, WHO ARE UNFAILINGLY SUPPORTIVE DESPITE SAYING THINGS LIKE "I DON'T REMEMBER THAT AT ALL" AND "CAN YOU PLEASE GET MY NOSE RIGHT?" (SORRY FOR NEVER GETTING YOUR NOSES RIGHT.) MARTIN AND LYNDA ROTHSTEIN, WHOSE YEARS OF LOVE AND LAUGHTER HAVE MADE OUR LIVES INFINITELY BETTER. LOPA, KIRAN, AND LEELA JACOB, FOR ADDING SANITY AND JOY TO THE BLOODLINE. ABBEY WESTBURY, FOR ALWAYS COMING THROUGH IN A CLUTCH. MARIE-HELENE BERTINO, ERIC BUNGE, GARNETTE CADOGAN, GARRETT CAREY, SUSAN FRECCIA, MIMI HOANG, AMANDA McBAINE, MIWA MESSER, NOA MEYER, HOLLY MORRIS, CHANI NICHOLAS, LISA ORRENIUS, AND DANI SHAPIRO, FOR SAYING THE RIGHT THING AT THE RIGHT MOMENT. PIYALI BHATTACHARYA, VERO GONZALEZ, ASHLEY M. JONES, AMANDA LEDUC, LISA NIKOLADAKIS, AND YACCAIRA SALVATIERRA, FOR COVENING AT HEDGEBROOK. BRITTANY K. ALLEN, BILL CHENG, ALEXANDER CHEE, LUIS JARAMILLO, TENNESSEE JONES, AND JULIA PHILLIPS, FOR BEING THE WRITING GROUP OF MY DREAMS.

MY AGENT, MICHELLE TESSLER, WHO SAID, "YOU SHOULD REALLY DRAW A BOOK," LIKE IT WAS A GOOD IDEA. (IT WAS A GOOD IDEA.)

MY EDITORS, CHRISTOPHER JACKSON AND VICTORY MATSUI, WHO SAID, "WHY?" AND, "NO, REALLY, WHY?" AND WHOSE VISION, HEART, AND CLARITY HELPED ME FIND MY OWN. NOAH EAKER, FOR TELLING ME NOT TO HOLD BACK. NICOLE COUNTS, CECIL FLORES, AND THE WHOLE ONE WORLD CREW, FOR MAKING THE BOOKS WE NEED. SUSAN KAMIL, ANDY WARD, AVIDEH BASHIRRAD, DHARA PARIKH, MARIA BRAECKEL, SARAH FEIGHTNER, BARBARA BACHMAN, AND BETH PEARSON, FOR HELP USHERING THIS BOOK INTO THE WORLD. RACHEL AKE, FOR THE EXTRAORDINARY COVER.

BOOK DOULA PETE FRIEDRICH AT PAGETURNER GRAPHIC NOVELS, FOR BEING UNFLAPPABLE AND REALLY NICE, EVEN WHEN WE'RE FIXING PICTURES AT 2 A.M. CINDY HO, FOR EARLY DESIGN HELP. PHOTOGRAPHERS SUSAN FRECCIA, KURT LEBECK, JOAN WEISSMAN, AND PHILIP WINN, FOR GETTING ME THE EXACT SHOTS I NEEDED. NELSON COLON, FOR FAST AND CAREFUL PICTURE RESEARCH.

KAVEH AKBHAR, SCOTT CHESHIRE, DURGA CHEW-BOSE, MAXWELL NEELY COHEN, PETER DESEVE, JOAN HILTY, MIKE HOUSTON, JOSH GONDELMAN, TED MINOFF, LYNN NOTTAGE, AND KRISTEN RADTKE, FOR HELP ALONG THE WAY.

THE HEDGEBROOK FOUNDATION, FOR CHANGING MY LIFE AND SO MANY OTHERS'. SULA'S ROOM, FOR THE GIFT OF TIME AND LODGING TO WRITE. POWDER KEG, FOR MY HAUNTED CARNIVAL WORKSPACE.

THE IMMIGRANT, MINORITY, AND MIXED-RACE FAMILIES STRUGGLING THROUGH EVERY DAY OF THIS AMERICA, FOR SHOWING ME HOW TO LIVE AND LOVE.

Z, FOR BEING WEIRDER AND FUNNIER AND MORE INTERESTING THAN I COULD EVER BEGIN TO CAPTURE ON THESE PAGES.

Image Credits

All photos and illustrations are by the author,
except for the following:

7, 14–15: Adobe Stock/Dario Bajurin

16: Aaron P. Bernstein/Getty Images

20: Adobe Stock/alb470

21 (top): Adobe Stock/Brian Weed

21 (bottom), 25, 39, 70 (top): Kurt Lebeck

23: Adobe Stock/vladimirzhoga

26–27: Adobe Stock/pomogayev

28: GRANGER/GRANGER—All rights reserved

36 (top), 38 (top), 223 (bottom): Adobe Stock/TheFinalMiracle

36 (bottom), 37 (middle right), 41, 132 (bottom): Adobe Stock/donyanedomam

37 (top left and top right): Adobe Stock/lamio

37 (bottom): Adobe Stock/SNEHIT

40 (top), 132 (middle): Adobe Stock/Iriana Shiyan

40 (bottom), 132 (top): Adobe Stock/Kailash Kumar

44 (top), 47: Adobe Stock/Tierney

49–52, 53 (top): Adobe Stock/sveta

53 (bottom, background), 55 (top, background), 55 (bottom, background), 61 (bottom, background), 231: Joan Weissman

53 (bottom), 55, 56, 59, 60, 61, 69 (car inserts): Greg Gjerdingen/Flickr/Creative Commons 2.0

56 (background), 59 (background), 60 (background): Shireen Jacob

57: Adobe Stock/MyLightscapes.com

58: Rob Laughter/Unsplash

68 (bottom): Adobe Stock/digerati

69 (top): Adobe Stock/Nomad_Soul

70 (bottom): Adobe Stock/Brian Scantlebury

75 (top): Adobe Stock/Peter Galbraith

80–85: Luke Stackpole/Unsplash

89 (top): Adobe Stock/olly

91–92: Adobe Stock/Colleen

93 (top): Adobe Stock/angelo.gi

93 (bottom), 94: Adobe Stock/zjk

98 (top): Adobe Stock/Ken

99, 101 (top): Susan Freccia

103, 115 (bottom): Adobe Stock/Yanukit

104–105: Adobe Stock/Artem

106 (top), 300 (right), 302 (right): Adobe Stock/pics721

106 (bottom right), 127 (top and bottom left), 133 (left), 135 (top and bottom left), 138 (bottom left), 139 (left), 143 (left), 144 (left): Yeo Khee/Unsplash

107: GALA Images ARCHIVE/Alamy Stock Photo

108–112, 119, 120–121, 137, 141, 145, 171: Phillip Winn

115 (top): Yonghyun Lee/Unsplash

117 (right), 133 (right): Casey Horner/Unsplash

125: Adobe Stock/Photodo51

126, 130–131, 142: Adobe Stock/Bruno Passigatti

128: Mike Wilson/Unsplash

129, 136, 140 (top): Adobe Stock/SkyLine

146–147: Alex Holyoake/Unsplash

148 (top): Manuel Pena/Unsplash

148 (bottom): Adobe Stock/blvdone

149: Photos courtesy of Jed Rothstein

151 (top): Renan Kamikoga/Unsplash

151 (bottom): Serge Lambotte/Unsplash

153, 154: Edi Libedinsky/Unsplash

157: Adobe Stock/Steve Lovegrove

158, 159 (right), 160, 162: iStock/JayLazarin

160, 162 (phone insets): Adobe Stock/Michael Felix

161: Ezra Shaw/Getty Images

163: AP Photo/Marty Lederhandler, File

164: Education Images/Universal Images Group North America LLC/Alamy Stock Photo

165: Spencer Platt/Getty Images

168 (top), 169, 205, 222: Adobe Stock/pavlofox

170: Rolf_52/Shutterstock.com

172: Adobe Stock/pikappa51

174: Adobe Stock/Oleksandr Dibrova

175, 176, 180, 181, 235 (bottom right): Adobe Stock/Morenovel

177–179: Spencer Platt/Getty Images

183–184: Ethan Hoover/Unsplash

185: Martin David/Unsplash

186, 192: Shutterstock/Kuprynenko Andrii

187, 188–189, 190–191, 192, 196, 198, 200, 201, 204, 206, 207–210: Adobe Stock/#moreideas

190 (man with money in thought bubble): Adobe Stock/© VadimGuzhva

194: Adobe Stock/Michelle

215: Adobe Stock/rmbarricarte

216 (top): Adobe Stock/Monkey Business

216 (bottom): Adobe Stock/Zeferli

217, 277, 309, 332: Adobe Stock/alex57111

218 (top): Elvert Barnes, Baltimore, Maryland, USA, CC BY-SA 2.0

218 (bottom), 219: Copyright © 2003 by David Monniaux, CC BY-SA 3.0

223 (middle), 250: Adobe Stock/Robert Elias

226–227, 240–241, 348–349: Juan/Pexels
227 (inset, people): Adobe Stock/Khorzhevska
227 (inset, bong): Adobe Stock/Josh Ross
232 (background): Adobe Stock/bradcalkins
232 (phone): MaxPixel.net
234 (top): Adobe Stock/goodmanphoto
235 (bottom left): Adobe Stock/Karen
236: Adobe Stock/sdecoret
238–239: Adobe Stock/Grigory Bruev
244: Pranay Pareek/Unsplash
245–249: Adobe Stock/dmindphoto
251 (top left), 255, 259, 263 (top and bottom): Adobe Stock/Yarek Gora
252, 262, 278 (right), 279 (right), 280 (top right): Adobe Stock/Kaziyeva-Dem'yanenko
253 (top): Adobe Stock/Stefano
253 (bottom), 256 (top and bottom), 258, 260, 261 (top): Adobe Stock/coralimages
255 (bottom): Adobe Stock/EpicStockMedia
257: Adobe Stock/rpbmedia
264 (top), 268, 269: Adobe Stock/Martijn Smeets
271, 272 (bottom), 273 (top): Naomi Hebert/Unsplash
272 (top): Adobe Stock/meredith1986
273 (bottom right): Adobe Stock/lichaoshu
288, 289 (top): Adobe Stock/Paul
296 (bottom): Adobe Stock/Rivison
302 (left): Adobe Stock/Tomasz Zajda
304 (top): Adobe Stock/dell
304 (bottom), 305–308: Adobe Stock/redswept
320–324: Adobe Stock/siv2203
325–330: Adobe Stock/goofyfoottaka
331: Photo by Jed Rothstein
338: Adobe Stock/danflcreativo
339–344: Adobe Stock/김대수 김대수
345: Adobe Stock/Mike Liu
346: Adobe Stock/Mary Lynn Strand
347: Adobe Stock/Rostislav Ageev

ABOUT THE AUTHOR

MIRA JACOB IS THE AUTHOR OF THE CRITICALLY ACCLAIMED NOVEL *THE SLEEPWALKER'S GUIDE TO DANCING,* WHICH WAS SHORTLISTED FOR INDIA'S TATA LITERATURE LIVE! FIRST BOOK AWARD FOR FICTION, HONORED BY THE ASIAN PACIFIC AMERICAN LIBRARY ASSOCIATION, AND NAMED ONE OF THE BEST BOOKS OF THE YEAR BY *THE BOSTON GLOBE, KIRKUS REVIEWS, BUSTLE,* AND *THE MILLIONS.* HER RECENT WORK HAS APPEARED IN *THE NEW YORK TIMES BOOK REVIEW, VOGUE, GLAMOUR, TIN HOUSE, ELECTRIC LITERATURE,* AND *LITERARY HUB.* SHE LIVES IN BROOKLYN.

MIRAJACOB.COM
TWITTER: @MIRAJACOB
INSTAGRAM: @GOODTALKTHANKS

New York City Subway
KNOCK KNOCK.
WHO'S THERE?
IGUANA.
IGUANA WHO?
IGUANA HOT SAUCE!
NOPE.